INDIAN ART
IN THE
ASHMOLEAN MUSEUM

INDIAN ART IN THE ASHMOLEAN MUSEUM

J. C. HARLE AND ANDREW TOPSFIELD

ASHMOLEAN MUSEUM
OXFORD 1987

British Library Cataloguing in Publication Data

Ashmolean Museum
Indian art in the Ashmolean Museum.
1. Art, Indic—Catalogs
I. Title II. Harle, J.C. and Topsfield, Andrew
III. Ashmolean Museum
709'.54'074 N7301

ISBN 0 907849 52 0 paperback
ISBN 0 907849 53 9 hardback

ASHMOLEAN MUSEUM PUBLICATIONS
EASTERN ART

Catalogue of Chinese Greenware
Chinese Ceramics
Eastern Ceramics from the Collection of
Gerald Reitlinger
Medieval Middle Eastern Pottery
Medieval Syrian Pottery
Oriental Lacquer
Treasures of the Ashmolean

Designed by Geoff Green
Set in Monophoto Photina, printed and bound
in Great Britain by Balding + Mansell UK Limited, Wisbech, Cambs. 1987

TABLE OF CONTENTS

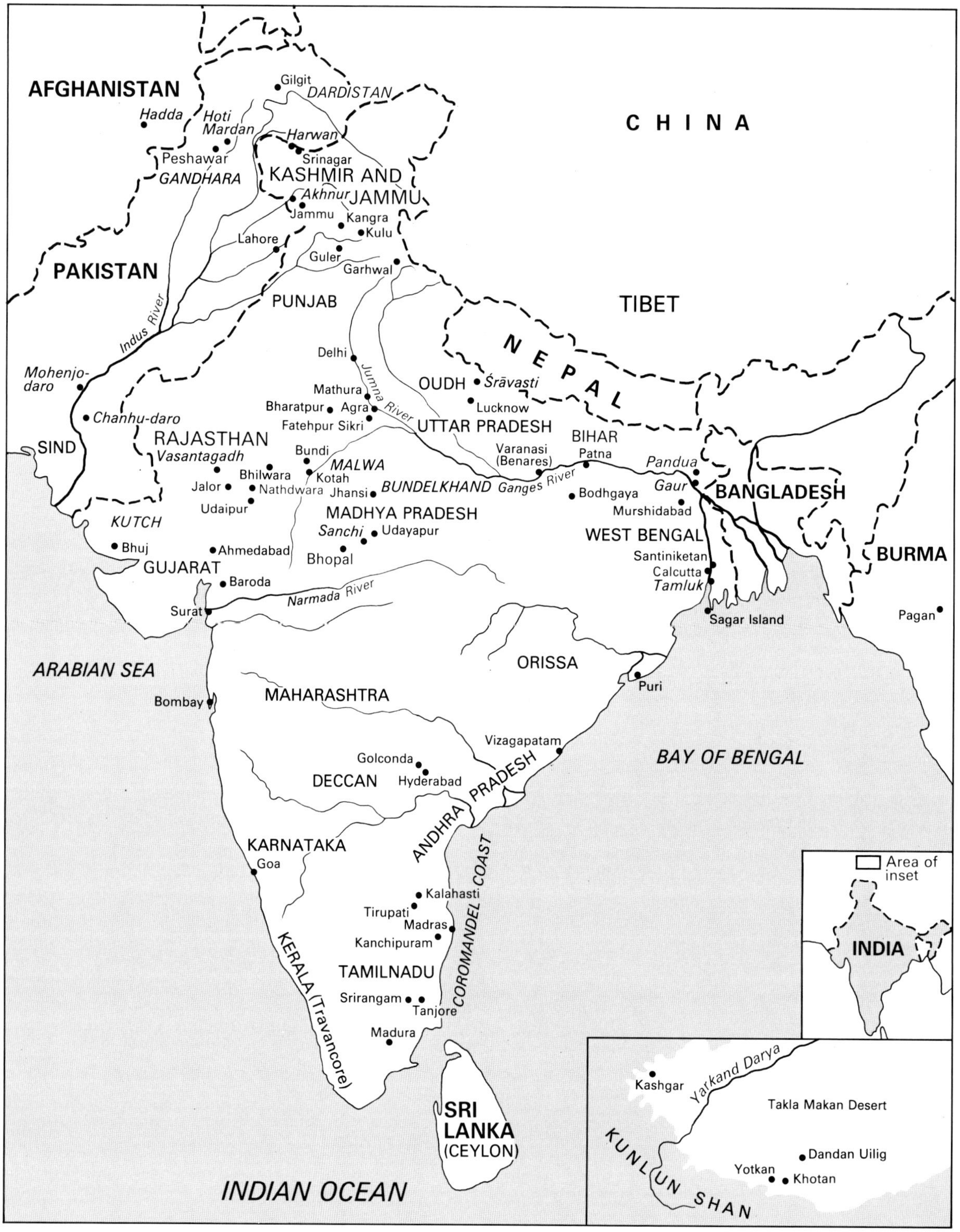

AFGHANISTAN
Hadda
Hoti Mardan
Peshawar
GANDHARA
Gilgit
DARDISTAN
Harwan
Srinagar
KASHMIR AND JAMMU
Akhnur
Jammu
Kangra
Kulu
Lahore
Guler
Garhwal
PAKISTAN
PUNJAB
CHINA
TIBET
NEPAL
Indus River
Mohenjo-daro
Chanhu-daro
SIND
Delhi
Jumna River
Mathura
Bharatpur
Agra
Fatehpur Sikri
OUDH
Śrāvasti
Lucknow
UTTAR PRADESH
RAJASTHAN
Vasantagadh
Bundi
MALWA
Kotah
Bhilwara
Jalor
Nathdwara
Udaipur
Jhansi
BUNDELKHAND
Ganges River
Varanasi (Benares)
BIHAR
Patna
Bodhgaya
Pandua
Gaur
BANGLADESH
Murshidabad
MADHYA PRADESH
KUTCH
Sanchi
Udayapur
Bhopal
Bhuj
Ahmedabad
GUJARAT
Baroda
WEST BENGAL
Santiniketan
Calcutta
Tamluk
BURMA
Narmada River
Surat
Sagar Island
Pagan
ARABIAN SEA
ORISSA
Puri
Bombay
MAHARASHTRA
Vizagapatam
BAY OF BENGAL
Golconda
Hyderabad
DECCAN
ANDHRA PRADESH
KARNATAKA
Goa
COROMANDEL COAST
Kalahasti
Tirupati
Madras
Kanchipuram
TAMILNADU
KERALA (Travancore)
Srirangam
Tanjore
Madura
SRI LANKA (CEYLON)
INDIAN OCEAN
Area of inset
INDIA
Kashgar
Yarkand Darya
Takla Makan Desert
KUNLUN SHAN
Dandan Uilig
Yotkan
Khotan

PREFACE

The Ashmolean Museum's holdings of Indian art are the most extensive in this country after the great London collections of the British Museum and the Victoria and Albert Museum, but they have not been widely known hitherto except through the publication of such famous masterpieces as the Tamluk terracotta (no.7) or Abu'l Hasan's drawing after Dürer (no.84). Our purpose in selecting objects for description in this handbook has been to provide an illustrated survey for visitors to the Museum's Indian galleries, reflecting the range and particular strengths of the collection, while also incorporating information and discussion of interest to scholars.

We are greatly indebted to Mr. Neil Kreitman for generous funding without which this book could not have been produced in anything like its present form. We also wish to thank many colleagues who assisted our work, including: Dr. F.R. Allchin, Dr. Mildred Archer, Mr. Douglas Barrett, Dr. G. Bhattacharya, Shri Lakshman Bhojak (L.D. Institute of Indology, Ahmedabad), Professor P. Chandra, Mr. M.A. Dhaky, Mr. Simon Digby, Mr. Toby Falk, Ms. Tapati Guhathakurta, Dr. O.R. Impey, Mr. Jonathan Katz, Dr. Simon Lawson, Professor T.S. Maxwell, Dr. Partha Mitter, Miss Veronica Murphy, Mr. Michael O'Keefe, Dr. M.S. Nagaraja Rao, Mr. Robert Skelton, Dr. John D. Smith, Miss Susan Stronge, Mr. Gerald Taylor, Miss Betty Tyers.

Miss Catherine Mortimer of the Laboratory for Archaeology and the History of Art, Oxford, made the metal analyses by X-ray fluorescence (XRF), Mrs. Geraldine Beasley of the Museum's staff undertook the photography, Mr. Bruce Graham helped with revision and editing and checked the inscriptions, and Miss Nora Addison typed the manuscript.

FURTHER READING

For general accounts of the development of Indian art and culture, the following are suggested:

D. Barrett and B. Gray, *Indian Painting*, repr. London 1978.

A.L. Basham, *The wonder that was India*, London, 3rd rev. ed; (paperback) 1985.

B. Gray ed., *The Arts of India*, Phaidon, Oxford, 1981.

J.C. Harle, *The Art and Architecture of the Indian Sub-Continent*, London, 1986.

S.L. Huntington, *The Art of Ancient India: Buddhist, Hindu, Jain*. New York etc., 1985.

HISTORY OF THE INDIAN COLLECTIONS

The Ashmolean first opened in its original building in Broad Street in 1683 and is thus the oldest public museum in England, and some claim, the world. The Founder's Collection presented by Elias Ashmole to the University was a traditional Cabinet of Curiosities or *Wunderkammer*, comprising a universal miscellany of rare or exotic objects and artefacts which had been largely accumulated by the Tradescants, John I and John II, the royal gardeners, in the first half of the 17th century. Along with rarities such as the remains of the Dodo and the American Indian chief Powhatan's "mantle", there were from the beginning a number of artefacts from the East Indies, mainly bows and other weapons which East India Company officials had no doubt brought back as curiosities.[1] Ashmole himself gave a fine pair of carved ebony chairs, said to have belonged to Charles II's queen, Catherine of Braganza, of a type made in Ceylon and South India under Dutch influence.[2] Other Indian donations occurred from time to time, notably Sir William Hedges' gift in c.1686–87 of a Pala image of Viṣṇu (no.48) which he had obtained on a visit to Sagar island in the Ganges delta. This is the earliest identifiable acquisition of a piece of Indian sculpture by any Western collection, just as the album of Indian paintings presented by Archbishop Laud to the Bodleian Library in 1640[3] is similarly the first known accession of its kind.

There was, however, never any attempt to collect or display Indian art in a representative manner. When in the late 19th century, after a long period of stagnation, the Ashmolean was regenerated and moved to its present site on Beaumont Street under the Keepership of Sir Arthur Evans (1884–1908), the inevitable rationalisation of the collections saw the transfer of the Indian material (including the Hedges Viṣṇu) to the ethnographical collections at the newly founded Pitt Rivers Museum. From this time the Ashmolean gained eminence as a museum of Western art and of archaeology, mainly Greco-Roman, Anglo-Saxon and Egyptian, while the art of Asia found little place in it as yet. The neglect of Indian art is hardly surprising in a period when even most Indologists, who had long lost the pioneering, humanistic sympathies of Sir William Jones and his late 18th century colleagues, denied the existence of any Indian fine art worthy of the name. Sir Monier Monier-Williams, Boden Professor of Sanskrit (1860–99), only voiced the received opinion of the age when he wrote, "... not a single fine large painting, nor beautiful statue is to be seen throughout India. Even the images of gods are only remarkable for their utter hideousness."[4] (He elsewhere gave conventional praise to the handicrafts of India, which since the Great Exhibition of 1851 had excited wide admiration.) It is ironic, therefore, that most of the Ashmolean's Indian

[1] A. MacGregor ed., *Tradescant's Rarities*, Oxford, 1983, nos.33–35, 51–52, 60–62, 68, 79–83; R.F. Ovenell, *The Ashmolean Museum 1683–1894*, Oxford, 1986.

[2] Also at Batavia: see J. Veenendaal, *Furniture from Indonesia, Sri Lanka and India during the Dutch period*, Delft, 1985, p.22. Ashmole's chairs are now displayed in the Founder's Room of the Museum.

[3] H.J. Stooke and K. Khandalavala, *The Laud Ragamala Miniatures*, Oxford, 1953; R. Skelton, "Indian art and artefacts in early European collecting", *The Origins of Museums*, O. Impey and A. MacGregor eds., Oxford, 1985.

[4] Sir M. Monier-Williams, *Brahmanism and Hinduism, or Religious thought and life in India*, 4th ed., London, 1891, p.469; for a history of Western appreciation of Indian art see P. Mitter, *Much Maligned Monsters*, Oxford, 1977.

collections, including a number of important sculptures,[5] were eventually to come to it from a museum founded by Monier-Williams as part of his Indian Institute, when the latter was dissolved in the post-imperial climate of the early 1960s. An account of the development of the present Indian collections must tell of the rise and fall of this institution.

The story of the Indian Institute, and particularly of its museum, is one of the high-minded, even sanctimonious, late Victorian ambitions of its founder over-reaching themselves and being gradually nullified by the inertia or sheer lack of funds of his successors.[6] The building itself, by Basil Champneys, with a gold elephant weather-vane and exterior carvings of an elephant, bull, lions and demi-gods, still commands the eastern end of Broad Street, though it now houses the History Faculty (earlier, the first English coffee house is believed to have stood on the same spot). It was erected by public subscription, much of the money coming from the princes and businessmen of India, which Monier-Williams had twice visited in 1875–76. The foundation stone was laid by the Prince of Wales in 1883, though shortage of funds was to prevent completion of the building until 1896. Its purpose, as reported by British and colonial newspapers, was "to house a complete collection of specimens of the products of India and a library of Indian literature and of books relating to India, as well as to be a centre of Oriental study and a meeting place for all who are interested in that portion of the Empire". The museum, an integral part of Monier-Williams' design, was to "present to the eye a typical collection of facts, illustrations and examples which . . . will give a concise synopsis of India – of the country and its material products – of the people and their moral condition".[7] As a museum of economic products, crafts and other artefacts viewed in an ethnographic light, it was clearly modelled to some extent on the vastly larger Indian Museum in South Kensington. The latter had recently been reconstituted through the amalgamation of the old East India Company museum in Whitehall with the growing collections of Indian craft objects at the South Kensington (later Victoria and Albert) Museum. A consolidation of these collections took place at the beginning of the 1880s when Caspar Purdon Clarke, a future Director of the Victoria and Albert, was sent to India on a buying expedition which yielded 3,400 acquisitions of almost every type and quality.[8]

Monier-Williams himself made a third fund-raising and collecting tour of India in the winter of 1883–84, arriving at Calcutta in time to take advantage of the International Exhibition then being held there, with its comprehensive displays of Indian products and artefacts. Besides obtaining some items from the Exhibition, he secured the help of the various regional authorities in assembling collections of local productions and shipping them to Oxford.[9] In each part of the sub-continent civil servants and museum officials carried out this commission as they thought best. The surviving lists of objects collected between 1883 and 1885 vary from compendious surveys of regional arts made by the most knowledgeable experts of the day to patchy and eccentric miscellanies.[10] The

5 Distinguished by accession numbers with an "O.S." or "X" prefix. Unfortunately no satisfactory records or register of accessions were kept in the Indian Institute Museum.

6 For an account of the Indian Institute and of Indian studies at Oxford see R. Symonds, *Oxford and Empire*, Oxford, 1986, ch.6; also R. Gombrich, *On being Sanskritic*, inaugural lecture, Oxford, 1978.

7 *Album of Indian Institute newspaper cuttings etc.*, Indian Institute Library F.a.4(9). See also *Record of the Establishment of the Indian Institute*, Oxford, 1897.

8 R. Desmond, *The India Museum 1801–1879*, London, 1982; R. Skelton, "The Indian Collections: 1798 to 1978", *Burlington Magazine* (Victoria and Albert Museum issue), May 1978, pp.297–304.

9 *Record of the Establishment of the Indian Institute*, pp.31, 33, 45–46: Monier-Williams acknowledges the help of the Viceroy (Lord Ripon), the Governors of Bombay and Madras and many officials, including F.S. Growse, Capt. R.C. Temple and Lockwood Kipling. For the Calcutta exhibition, see *Official Report of the Calcutta International Exhibition*, 2 vols., Calcutta, 1885.

10 *Indian Institute Museum: Original Lists*, MS volume in the Department of Eastern Art, Ashmolean Museum.

The Indian Institute Museum with its original display, c.1898–99.

Madras Museum dispatched several hundred selected examples of southern domestic and ritual metalwares, ornaments, textiles, lacquer and woodwork etc. From Bengal came a similar representative collection of handicrafts, devotional images, folk paintings and economic products, scientifically catalogued under fifteen headings by Babu T.N. Mukharji.[11] A further wide selection of objects, including the Umā-Maheśvara sculpture (no.45) and a good collection of musical instruments,[12] was presented by Sir Sourindro Mohun Tagore of Calcutta. In Rajputana the Jeypore Museum Committee (Hon. Sec. T.H. Hendley) organised the collection of over four hundred objects at a cost of Rs. 2000, including some contemporary Jaipur paintings and a quantity of arms and armour presented by the Maharaja. From the Punjab it was reported, "Baden Powell is making collections." The Municipalities of Moradabad presented a range of local metalwares. From the Central Provinces came saris and textiles, female ornaments and weapons "used by wild tribes in the Chhatisgarh hills". From Dacca came muslin, from Ajmer a model cobra, from Travancore three blown crocodile eggs, three tailor-bird nests and a granite stone used in scrubbing elephants.

It must have been realised early on that this ambitious accumulation would present display problems in the limited gallery space proposed for the uncompleted Institute

[11] Babu T.N. Mukharji, *List of Articles collected for the Oxford Institute under the instruction of T.W. Holderness Esq. and Dr George Watt*, Calcutta, 1884 (36 pp.), bound in the *Original Lists* MS volume (n.10 above). In the Paintings section of this consignment are listed many of the Kalighat pictures which are still held by the Indian Institute Library (see H.J. Stooke, 'Kalighat Paintings in Oxford', *Indian Art and Letters*, n.s.XX, 2, 1946, pp.71–73; also W.G. Archer, *Bazaar paintings of Calcutta*, London, 1953, pls.16, 17, 20–25).

[12] Some of these are now displayed in the new musical galleries of the Pitt Rivers Museum.

building. When Babu T.N. Mukharji was commissioned to catalogue the collections in 1886 (a job which he was unable to finish),[13] he described the eventual aim of the collection as "to convey instruction" rather than to "make an effective show". Ten years later the Institute was finally opened and, with the aid of a grant from the University, the installation of its Museum was carried out by Dr. H. Lüders, assisted by Mr. Long of the Pitt Rivers Museum, and completed in 1898. A series of contemporary photographs of interior views of the Institute must have been taken soon after.[14] The main Museum hall, on the first floor of the building, and its ambulatory with columns supporting an upper gallery with *jālī*-work balustrades (fig.1) are shown chockablock with heavy wooden cases crammed inside and below with exhibits (a concentrated mode of display still happily preserved today at the Pitt Rivers). The cases are arranged by region and prominently labelled with the names of individual and corporate donors. Rugs and *darīs* cover the floors, diverse weapons are fixed to the walls and columns, and life-like Indian costumed dummies stand guard. An entrance corridor contains several small *stūpas* from Bodhgaya (no.47) as well as other sculptures and rugs, a model of the emperor Humayun's tomb (presented by the Maharaja of Alwar) and what appears to be a stuffed yak.

In 1899 Monier-Williams died and to his less enthusiastic successors the Museum became, one suspects, something of a white elephant. The main problem was that no financial provision had been made for its proper running by a full-time curator. Its Keeper was *ex officio* the Boden Professor of Sanskrit. This was hardly satisfactory, since apart from their natural distraction by other duties, those individuals with the advanced philological aptitudes required by such a position proved (with the single exception of Prof. Johnston) to be impervious to the visual arts of India. At the regular meetings of the Curators of the Institute the problems of the Museum took second place to discussions about the state of the Library.[15] Nevertheless a wide range of objects offered by ex-I.C.S. officers and other India hands continued to be accepted in most cases. These included a collection of antiquities given by Mr. Robert Sewell (1899); 23 Gandhara sculptures from the Rev. Murray-Aynsley (1911) and others from Miss Barlow (1912–25); a group of Kashmir knitted gloves and stockings, said to have belonged to Warren Hastings, from Mr. J.R. Harris (1933) and the Luard collection of brass images in 1936 (nos. 57, 71). Occasional loans of objects were made to exhibitions in London and elsewhere.

There was little steady policy concerning the Museum, but sporadic reappraisals of its aims were usually followed by dispersals of unwanted parts of the collections. This process had already begun in 1899–1900 with the transfer of the entomological and zoological collections to the University Museum and the sale of some sets of animal horns. In 1909 a most trenchant critique of the Museum was made by Lord Curzon, then Chancellor of the University, whose Viceroyalty had been distinguished by his keen interest in the upkeep of India's monuments and museums.[16] Recommending the

[13] T.N. Mukharji, *Catalogue of Articles at the Indian Museum, Oxford*, MS volume, 1886, in the Department of Eastern Art, Ashmolean Museum. Mukharji subsequently wrote *Art-manufactures of India*, Calcutta, 1888, a very useful survey compiled for the Glasgow International Exhibition of that year.

[14] Monier-Williams papers, Bodleian Library. I am grateful to Mr. Jonathan Katz, Indian Institute Librarian, for bringing these photographs to my attention and for much other information; also to Mrs. M. de Goris for a guided tour of the Indian Institute in which she formerly worked.

[15] *Minutes of the Curators of the Indian Institute*, 3 MS vols., University Archives, Bodleian Library. I am grateful to Miss Ruth Vyse for making these available to me, and to the Keeper of the Archives, University of Oxford, for permission to quote from them.

[16] Lord Curzon, "The Indian Institute", printed Confidential Note, 25 March 1909, bound in *Minutes*, vol.2 (n.15 above).

removal of the Museum from the overcrowded Institute, he criticised Monier-Williams' "too grandiose conception", which

> bore no real relation to the needs either of the Institute or of Oxford. No Indian student who comes to Oxford requires to see a meagre and ill-assorted collection of some of the commonest objects in his native country; to him the display must appear mean and contemptible. But equally can no English student – or candidate for the Indian Civil Service – gain the remotest idea of India by an examination of the scanty models, fabrics, carvings or products here displayed. If an English student of India wishes to study either her ethnology or her art in an exhibition, he must go to South Kensington . . . [The Museum collection] has remained almost stationary for a number of years, and, as the figures of admission show, is visited annually by more women than men – a sufficient condemnation of its continued retention here, and a pathetic commentary upon Sir M. Monier-Williams's assurance that it was not intended to attract "mere sight-seers, curiosity-hunters and excursionists."

It is scarcely a coincidence that the following month the Curators resolved on a policy of gradual dispersal of the collections "by transference, so far as possible, to other University institutions". But little was done about this at the time. Instead, for several years after 1912 an active Museum Committee led by Mr. Vincent Smith, the author of standard histories of India and its art, supervised the improvement and relabelling of the display. In 1922 a short handbook to the Institute by Prof. Macdonell, with a summary catalogue of the Museum by Mr. A. Rost, was prepared but never published.[17] Then in 1926 a peevish note reappeared in the Curators' deliberations. It was remarked that in one quarter "167 persons (for the most part school children and Americans) had visited the Museum" and it was further decided to get rid of certain "positively injurious" stuffed animals. Later the entire contents of the Museum were offered for transfer to the Pitt Rivers but were refused for lack of space. Nevertheless, many objects, including the Jaipur arms and armour, did pass to the Pitt Rivers during the next few years.

Under the Keepership of Prof. E.H. Johnston (1937–42) a brief Indian summer occurred. Unlike his predecessors he appreciated the qualities of Indian art and purchased examples of Mathura sculpture, including the superb Śiva head (no.24). He arranged a new display of sculpture in the Museum's main hall (fig.2), discussing the problems he encountered in a published article.[18] Almost at once, however, the outbreak of war and the appropriation of the Institute for other purposes caused the Museum to close. In 1945 the Curators once again questioned the purpose of the Museum and decided against its immediate restoration. But a solution appeared in the following year when they approved a proposal made by Dr. William Cohn, a distinguished war-time refugee from Berlin, that the Indian collections should be amalgamated with the Ashmolean's Chinese ceramic collections in a new Museum of Eastern Art. This Museum opened in the Institute in 1949 under the direction of Dr. Cohn and later of Mr. Peter Swann (1955–66). A number of Indian acquisitions were made in this period, including the purchase in 1960 of some Mughal and Deccani paintings. In 1957 further "useless and unnecessary" Indian material was disposed of.

By this time the Indian Institute was already under threat. With the disappearance of its imperial and I.C.S. connections, it was regarded by the powers within the University as a redundant and moribund institution, occupying a desirable site for the erection of a new administrative block (this was eventually built elsewhere). In the early 1960s the Institute was abolished and its Library was later reincarnated above the New Bodleian

[17] Kept with Mukharji's MS volume (n.13 above) in the Department of Eastern Art.

[18] E.H. Johnston, "Methods of displaying Indian sculpture", *The Museums Journal*, vol.39, Dec. 1939, pp.389–93.

The Indian Institute Museum after rearrangement by Prof. E.H. Johnston in 1939 (from *Museums Journal*, vol.39, pl.XLVIII).

building, where, merged with the Bodleian Indian holdings, it is now one of the finest Indological libraries in the world.[19] The Museum collections had meanwhile moved in 1962 to their present home at the Ashmolean in the newly established Department of Eastern Art.

During the last twenty-five years, despite the scarcity of funds available to a University museum, there has been a steady flow of acquisitions of Indian sculpture, painting and decorative arts, and the overall balance of the collections has been consolidated and improved. Major purchases of recent years include the Mathura coping (no.10), the Gupta *makara* (no.26), the Harwan plaque (no.27), the post-Gupta ceiling slab (no.32) and the Mughal floral carpet (no.100). For many acquisitions, however, the Department has been indebted to a number of generous donors, including Mr. Oswald J. Couldrey, Mr. E.M. Scratton, Mr. and Mrs. Douglas Barrett and the late Mr. Gerald Reitlinger, who along with his munificent gift of Eastern ceramics presented a small group of important and beautiful Indian paintings (nos. 82–84, 89, 92).

A.T.

[19] J. Katz, "The Indian Institute Library, Oxford, and its Bodleian hosts", *South Asia Library Group Newsletter*, 26, June 1985.

COLOUR PLATES

1. No.5. Rhyton. Found near Gilgit, 3rd–1st century B.C.

2. No.7. *Yakṣī* or mother goddess. Tamluk, c.200 B.C.

3. No.10. Coping of a sandstone railing. Mathura(?), first half of 1st century A.D.

4. No.24. Head of Śiva. Mathura, early 5th century A.D.

5. No.32. Ceiling slab with eight armed men. Northern Gujarat or Southern Rajasthan, c.750 A.D.

6. No.33. Lokeśvara – Padmapāṇi. Attributed to the Punjab, 6th–8th century A.D.

7. No.46. Standing Buddha. Probably Bodhgaya, 10th–11th century.

8. No.52. Gaṇeśa. Orissa, 16th century.

9. No.64. Nandī. Deccan or South India, 16th–17th century.

10. No.77. Portable Viṣṇu shrine. Tirupati, late 18th or early 19th century.

11. No.79. The Jagannātha trio. Puri, Orissa, c.1900(?).

12. No.80. Hanumān. Kalighat, Calcutta, c.1870.

13. No.82. Hamza overthrows 'Amr-i Ma'dī Kariba. Mughal, c.1562–65.

14. (slightly enlarged) No.85. Sultan 'Abdullah Qutb Shah. Golconda, c.1640.

15. (slightly enlarged) No.86. Lovers by a lotus pool.
Deccan or Rajasthan, c.1700.

16. No.88. Kamodanī *rāgiṇī*. Bundi or Kotah, c.1770.

17. No.90. Mahārāṇa Bhīm Siṅgh with a hawk. Udaipur, c.1815–20.

18. No.91. Bāz Bahādur and Rūpmatī. Kulu, c.1720.

19. No.98. Casket overlaid with mother-of-pearl. Gujarat, c.1590–1600.

20. No.94. Sarus crane. By Shaikh Zain ud-Dīn. Calcutta. c.1780–82.

21. No.96. Śakuntalā writing a love-letter. By Ravi Varma, c.1880–85.

22. No.97. Kṛṣṇa and Rādhā. By Ishwari Prasad, c.1910.

23. No.99. *Scrutore* (writing cabinet). Sind(?), early 17th century.

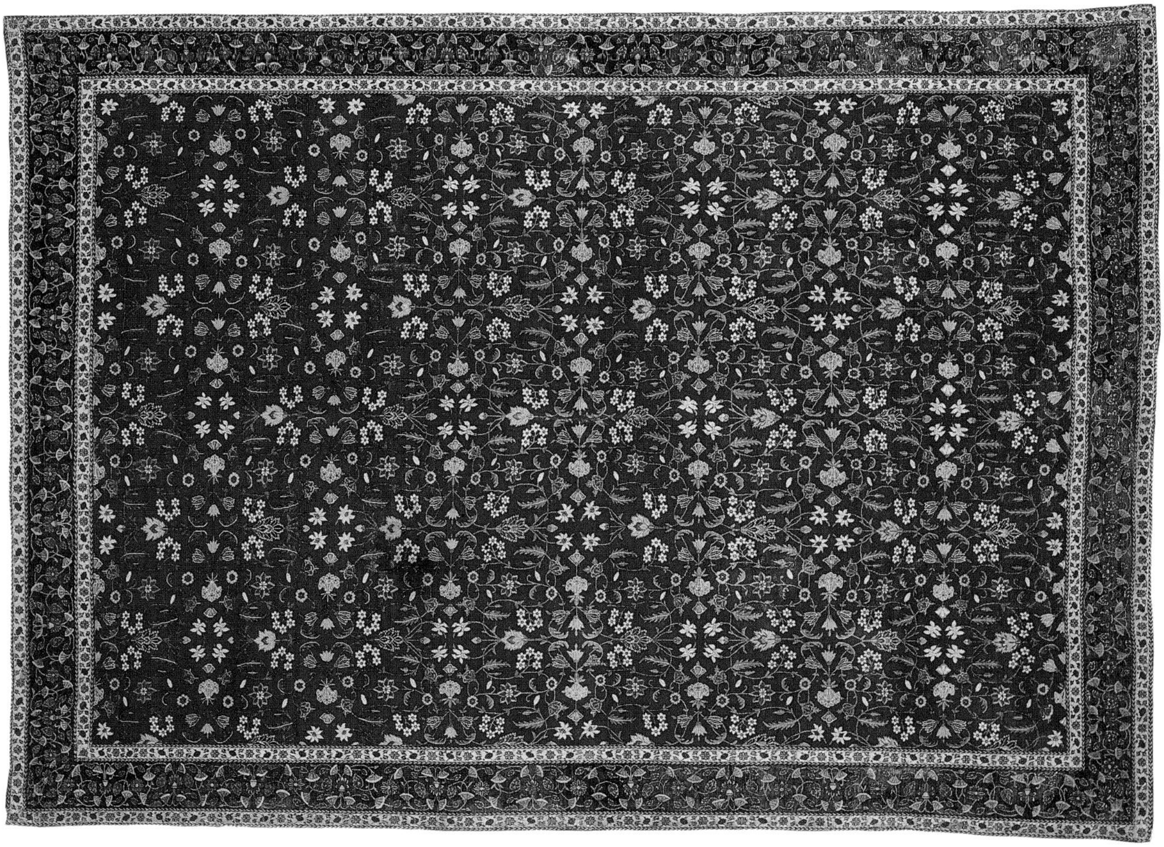

24. No.100. Floral carpet. Mughal, early 18th century.

HINDU, BUDDHIST AND JAIN SCULPTURE

1

Triangular prism sealing, terracotta. Mohenjo-Daro, Sind, Pakistan, c.2000 B.C.

Length 1 in. (3.3 cm.)
Md 013
Purchased 1941 with the help of the Max Müller Memorial Fund

The Indus or Harappan civilisation, whose mature period dated from roughly 2550 B.C. to 1750 B.C., is known exclusively from excavated sites located over a wide band of territory running some 300 miles to both east and west of the present India-Pakistan border, from the Punjab to the Arabian Sea. In spite of a complexity of urban development at the two largest sites, Mohenjo-daro and Harappa, not reached elsewhere until much later times, remains of artistic interest are rare, with the exception of little terracotta and steatite sculptures of animals, notably bulls. Of even greater artistic merit are the animal figures, along with short inscriptions in the as yet undeciphered script, on the steatite seals found in great numbers. These prefigure the great skill and sympathy in depicting animals which the Indian artist has never failed to show over the ages during the long course of Indian art. Datings of the civilisation, originally made from Mesopotamian parallels, are now based on calibrated radiocarbon tests.

Sealings (the impress made by the seal) such as this one are much rarer than seals. On one face of the prism a male figure sits on a throne or dais, in a "yogic" pose. Several seals show a figure seated in a similar way: one of the most elaborate and best known of these, probably animal-headed and ithyphallic, and with a horned headdress, sits surrounded by animals, prompting an identification as a proto-Śiva in a form known as Paśu-pati, "lord of beasts". This designation is only attested in the historical period, but it has been adduced as one of the principal pieces of evidence for a direct link between the religion of the Indus civilisation and later Hinduism. While some other aspects of the civilisation do suggest such a link, what may have been provision for ritual bathing, for example, and the presence of fire-altars, it has not been proved. What has not been pointed out, moreover, is that the "yogic" pose of all these Indus civilisation figures, with the feet placed sole to sole, is indeed employed in yoga but is rarely depicted in later Indian sculpture (see no.52).

The Ashmolean's figure is flanked by a gharial and a fish on one side; what appears on the other side cannot be distinguished. Another facet has five characters in the Indus script. The third bears a bull-like animal.

PUBLISHED

D. Srinivasan, "The so-called Proto-Śiva seal from Mohenjo-Daro: An Iconological Assessment", *Archives of Asian Art*, XXIX (1975–6), pp.55–6, figs. 13–15.

2

Two bulls (oxen?), terracotta. Chanhu-daro, Sind, Pakistan, c.2200 B.C.

Left Ch 01 – $3\frac{5}{8}$ in. (9.3 cm.)
Right Ch 04 – $2\frac{1}{2}$ in. (6.4 cm.)

These two toy figures of bulls, crude as they are in comparison to the animals depicted on some of the seals, already show some of the plastic sense as well as the sympathy for animals which have always characterised the Indian modeller and sculptor. Although straight backed cattle were already known in Harappan times, these appear to have been modelled

on the typical Indian breed (*bos indicus*) with its hump, only traces of which remain, however, on these little animals. The larger (left) has a neatly drilled hole through its neck. It was probably one of a pair, and the hole allowed one of the small terracotta bullock carts, many of which have been found at Harappan sites, to be attached; it also suggests that the modeller had oxen in mind. The set of the horns on both animals supports this. The smaller (right) has pellet eyes.

Chanhu-daro is an important Harappan site some 75 miles (120 km.) south of Mohenjodaro. According to the excavator, bulls with drilled holes for attaching little carts are not found at the latter site while the front and rear legs joined together, as in the pair illustrated, are only found there at the earlier levels.

LITERATURE

E.J.H. Mackay, *Chanhu-daro Excavations*, New Haven, Conn., 1941, pp.155, 165; pl.LVIII, 22.

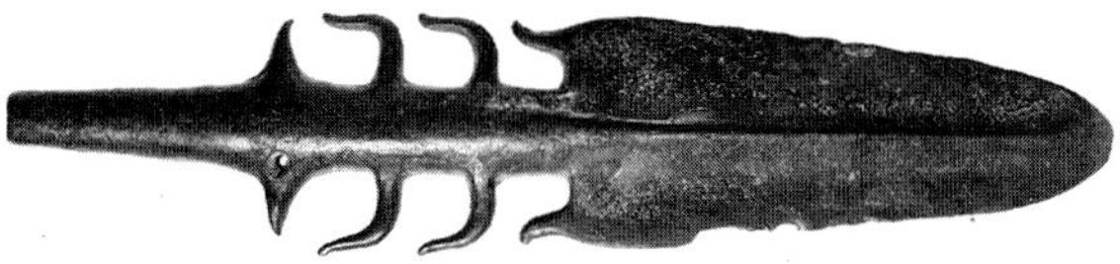

3

Harpoon, copper, cast in a mould. Probably from eastern Uttar Pradesh, c.2500–1000 B.C.

Height 11¾ in. (29.8 cm.)
1986.13
Gift of Douglas and Mary Barrett

Copper objects in the form of weapons, tools and implements have been found at sites scattered over most of India and Pakistan but those indicating a "separate cultural identity", in the Allchins' phrase, a group to which the harpoon belongs, tend to come from the Doab, between the Jumna and the Ganges and sites to the south and east; harpoons themselves have only been found in the Doab and at closely adjacent sites. They have nearly always been found in hoards (deposits of coins or other objects purposely concealed and usually buried). The Museum also possesses a celt or axe head (1954–66 – donated by Major General H.L. Haughton) from the largest of all these hoards, the mammoth deposit of 400 copper objects, accompanied by some silver, weighing in all 829 lbs. (376 kg.), found at Gungeria in Madhya Pradesh. The find-place of this harpoon is not known. The small lug or eyelet was to enable the head to be detached from the shaft and secured by a line.

The relation of the "Copper hoard culture" to better known ones still presents problems although certain associations have made it possible to assign approximate dates to it. The principal uncertainty about the copper hoard objects remains their use; their excessive weight and often size would point to a non-utilitarian use, ritual perhaps or as objects of exchange or status symbols.

LITERATURE

P. Yule, *Metalwork of the Bronze Age in India*, Munich, 1985; see also B. and R. Allchin, *The Rise of Civilisation in India and Pakistan*, Cambridge, 1982; Colonel A. Bloomfield, I.A., *Extraordinary Finds of Indian Copper Implements*, Saxmundham, Suffolk, n.d.

4

Two animal heads (ungulates), terracotta. Motamuri, Andhra, 7th (?) century B.C. to 2nd century A.D. or later.

Length 4½ in. (11.5 cm.) and 5½ in. (14 cm.)
X.235, X.236

The Museum has a collection of megalithic wares from several sites near Hyderabad in Andhra, excavated in the 2nd and 3rd decades of this century by E.H. Hunt and belonging to what is termed the South Indian Iron Age or Megalithic Grave Complex. While iron age graves in Andhra and Tamilnadu characterised by the megalithic wares have been extensively investigated, they have been marked by an almost total absence of the terracottas depicting humans and animals which are such a common feature of the early historical period in India. This may be due, of course, to the fact that very few settlements, as opposed to graves, have been excavated. These two heads, which must have belonged to complete animals, appear to be unique.

The heads portrayed are of quite different animals. The one on the left would appear to be an antelope,

with its relatively pointed head and straight swept-back horns. The other has a highly distinctive appearance and since there appear to be no other examples in pre-historic or early Indian art, one must assume that the animal was known to the modeller. With its straight-sided jaw and raised nasal region, indicating what appears to be an abnormally large nasal cavity, there is a striking resemblance between the animal depicted and a saiga (*Saiga tatarica*) of S.E. Russia and parts of Central Asia.

PUBLISHED

E.H. Hunt, "Hyderabad Cairn Burials and their significance", *Journal of the Royal Anthropological Institute*, vol.LIV, fig.1, pp.140–56. "Heads of rams"; Laurence S. Leshnik, *South Indian "Megalithic" Burials*, Wiesbaden, 1974, figs. 40–3 & 4.

LITERATURE

Grzimek's *Animal Life Encyclopedia*, Ed. B. Grzimek, New York, 1972, vol.13: Mammals IV, pp.448–57, iii. and R.M. Nowak & J.L. Paradiso: *Walker's Mammals of the World* (4th Ed.) 2 vols., Baltimore, 1983, vol.2, p.1288, illus. p.1289.

5 COLOUR PLATE I

Rhyton in the form of a centaur, bronze, solid cast; the vessel (heavily restored) is hammered. Found near Imit, Ishkoman valley, near Gilgit, Pakistan, 3rd – 1st century B.C.

Height $10\frac{5}{8}$ in. (26.9 cm.)
1963.28 (formerly Dept. of Antiquities, 1954.159.)
Presented by the Executors of the late Sir Aurel Stein

This rhyton and a small bronze bowl or ladle with a projecting horse's head (1976.122, also transferred from the Dept. of Antiquities) are, with the exception of a copper hoard harpoon (no.3) and axe-head, the oldest metal objects from the Indian subcontinent in the Museum. Discovered when a portion of hillside fell

away, they are also exceptional in that their find-place is accurately documented.

The vigorously but rather crudely modelled solid cast figure of a bearded centaur derives from Graeco-Roman models. The small animal, an ibex, is held between the centaur's hands by a pin centrally located through its body, allowing the little animal to remain horizontal while the rhyton is tilted by the drinker, who received his beverage through the centaur's male organ. Animal rhytons, sometimes simply terminating in animal heads (see no.18), can be traced back to Achaemenid times.

A recent metal analysis (see below) suggests that the two objects come from quite different cultures and, as part of a hoard, which seems highly likely, may have been made at a considerable distance in time one from the other. The little bowl is almost exclusively copper; the rhyton is a leaded bronze of the type (although the lead content is very high) common in much of the ancient world in the centuries before and after the beginning of our era. There may, of course, have been other objects in the hoard, which were not turned over to the authorities, those in precious metals in particular.

A solid link has been established between the small bowl and graves in the Pamirs in Tadjikistan, U.S.S.R., of the late centuries B.C. Very similar, but entirely zoomorphic rhytons in terracotta, on the other hand have been found at sites in ancient Bactria, dating from Kuṣāṇa times. This tallies with the generally accepted assumption that the forms of metal wares subsequently give rise to terracotta analogues, rather than vice-versa, and would tend to place the rhyton in the last two or three centuries B.C. It has further been suggested by Professor Jettmar (correspondence) that rather than being part of a local magnate's treasure imported into Dardistan, the ancient name of the region where they were found, the Museum's two objects were part of the ritual equipment of a tribe, the "Horse-people" of the ancient sources (Skt. Aśvakayana, Grk. Assakenoi) who ruled over the mountains west of Tibet.

METAL ANALYSES

Rhyton: Iron: 0.42; Nickel: 0.13; Copper: 68.0; Arsenic: 0.66; Lead: 23.1; Tin: 7.1.
Bowl: Iron: traces; Copper: 99+; Tin: traces.

PUBLISHED

Sir A. Stein, "Archaeological Notes from the Hindukush Region", *Journal of the Royal Asiatic Society*, 1944, pp.14–16 and pl. IIIa.

LITERATURE

K. Jettmar, "The Middle Asiatic Heritage of Dardistan (Islamic Collective Tombs in Punyal and their Background)", *East and West*, 17, nos.1–2 (1967), pp.59–79; K.A. Abdullaev & V.A. Zavyalov, "Vessels on Zoomorphic Pedestals from Settlements of Kushanic Bactria" (in Russian) *Soviet Archaeology*, no.1, 1985, pp. 202–11.

6

Female figure, terracotta. Northwest Province, Pakistan, c.200 B.C.–200 A.D.

Height $6\frac{1}{4}$ in. (15.8 cm.)
1958.3
E.M. Scratton Gift

Hand-modelled figurines such as this, with pinch noses, split pellet eyes and crude appliqué representations of headdress and ornaments, are found in abundance in the region around Peshawar, Pakistan. Some were found at nearby Chārsada by the excavator, Sir Mortimer Wheeler, who gave them the somewhat inappropriate name of "baroque ladies". From scientifically conducted excavations, they are securely dated from around 200 B.C. to c.200 A.D. (Dani, pp.46ff., pl.XXIV–XXVII). The buttocks (rear view) are voluptuously rounded in a naturalistic style, in striking contrast to the schematised front view. The larger group to which these figures belong, all distinguished by this primitive technique, have been found at chalcolithic period settlements from as far west as eastern Iran and variants are still made as toys in present day Bengal. It is doubtful whether the majority of these figures, even in early times, can be dignified with the name of mother-goddesses.

LITERATURE

Sir Mortimer Wheeler, *Chārsada, A Metropolis of the North-West Frontier*, being a report on the excavations of 1958, Oxford, 1962. A.H. Dani et al. "Shaikhan Dheri Excavation." *Ancient Pakistan* 2 (1965–66), pp. 17–214.

7

COLOUR PLATE 2

A *yakṣī* or mother goddess, terracotta, moulded plaque. Tamluk, the ancient Tamralipti, c.200 B.C.

Height 8 in. (21.3 cm.)
X.201

Through the ages, terracotta has formed the medium for some of India's most important and beautiful sculpture (see, for example, nos.26, 28, 50). One distinctly Indian type, although probably ultimately derived from western Asia, is the small upright plaque bearing a single moulded figure, usually a woman, or more rarely a couple, man and woman (*mithuna*). The so-called "Oxford plaque" is the finest and best preserved of these plaques which have been found at many sites in northern India, from the north-west to Bengal. The female figures are distinguished by certain common features of dress: a huge bi- or tricornate headdress, the large bolster-like ear-rings and the massive tubular bracelets. Strangely enough, these articles of dress appear on contemporary metal effigies of women (no.9) but never on stone reliefs.

The Oxford terracotta is also exceptional, in that both the exact location and the time of its finding, in 1883, are recorded, long before similar but fragmentary examples surfaced in excavations in the same area near Calcutta after World War II and revealing by their identical style that here was a distinct Bengali sub-style. The beauty of this plaque lies largely in the exquisite fineness of detail made possible by impression on a faultless matrix of well-levigated clay. After impression by the mould, doubtless also of terracotta, details like the rosettes on the ground were added by *poinçon* and the lines indicating drapery scratched on. Some of the detail, such as the deer and *makara* buckles on the sash across the figure's torso, while perfectly executed are so small they can hardly be seen by the naked eye. A *makara* is a mythical monster (see no.26). Aesthetically, there is a curious contrast between the figure's plump and sensuously modelled arms and her stick-like legs, while the general air of barbaric splendour is quite outside the mainstream of Indian art.

Various identifications have been proposed for this and similar figures. One of these is a *yakṣī*, the female counterpart of a *yakṣa* or local godling. At one level they are simply women wearing the finery of royal or high-born ladies of the time and it is known from stone reliefs that male figures without any particularly distinguishing attribute could represent Hindu gods or great figures of early Buddhist story. On the other hand, it is possible that they represent mother-goddesses, whose cult was widespread; their veneration at a popular level would account for the large number of these plaques. A terracotta of a pregnant woman (seated) wearing a bi-cornate headdress from the north-west in the Peshawar Museum further suggests such an identification.

PUBLISHED

G. Bysach, "Note on some copper coins and a terracotta figure", *Proc. As. Soc. of Bengal for 1888*. S. Kramrisch, "Indian Terracottas", *J.I.S.O.A.* VII, 1939, pp.88–110. Report of Curators of Indian Institute for 1938–39. E.H. Johnston, *Annual Bibliography of Indian Archaeology for the Year 1939*. vol.XII, p.16, pl.V., (also E.H. Johnston, *J.I.S.O.A.*, vol.X, 1942, pp.94–102) who attributes the piece to Kausambī. S.K. Saraswati, *Yearbook of the Royal Asiatic Society of Bengal for 1949*, pp.174–5; *Early Sculpture of Bengal*, Calcutta, 1962, pp.96–102, particularly Ch.8, n.9. B. Durrans and R. Knox, *India: Past into Present*, Exhib. Cat., British Museum, London, 1982, p.47. A.G. Poster, *From Indian Earth: 4,000 Years of Terracotta Art*, Brooklyn, 1986, pp.22–3, fig.2. J.C. Harle, *The Art and Architecture of the Indian Sub-Continent*, London, 1986, p.38, fig.24.

8

Heads and busts of terracotta figurines. Mathura, c.200 B.C.

Average width (of heads): $1\frac{1}{4}$ in. (3.2 cm.)
X.193–200.

Terracottas of this type, of a characteristic grey colour, have been found in great numbers at Mathura and its environs, though complete figures are very rare. The grey colour is due to a particular firing technique, not to the clay from which they are made: X.196 (top right), for instance, is the usual terracotta colour. The major excavations of the 1960s and 70s at Sonkh, near Mathura, conducted jointly by Professor Härtel for the Free University of Berlin and the Archaeological Survey of India, uncovered a number of these terracotta figures or heads in scientifically determined strata, resulting in a firm dating of c.200 B.C.

In technique, these figurines represent a half-way stage between the entirely hand-modelled type, with appliqué decoration seen in no.6, and the entirely moulded form of no.7. Here only the face and hair are from a mould. These little terracottas have been widely assumed to be mother goddesses; the presence of what are almost certainly male heads in this group challenges this rather simplistic identification. The male heads are recognisable by portions of turban (?) and a different treatment of the hair.

PUBLISHED

M. Neff, "Some Indian Terracottas at Oxford", *Oriental Art*, N.S. II, 2, pp.56–59.

9

Female figure, bronze. Northwest India or Pakistan, c.100 A.D.

Height $3\frac{15}{16}$ in. (10 cm.)
1973.7

This little figure is immediately recognisable by her pose and highly characteristic headdress as the same depicted on many moulded terracotta plaques (see no.7). The "bi-cornate" headdress is the same, even including the pins stuck into it (on both sides here). Even the large cylindrical ear-rings, one shown head on, the other in three-quarter view are the same; so are the large tubular wristlets and the sensuous modelling of the plump arms. Certain details of costume differ significantly, however. There is no sign of the elaborate metal or jewelled girdle: the light belt, the tassels and the long sash suspended from it on the right side are quite different, as are the necklaces. From the rear it is clear that the woman held drapery in her left hand. All these features suggest an origin in the north-west of the sub-continent, as does the sensuous modelling of the hips seem from the rear, and indeed there is an almost identical figure from Bannu, southwest of Peshawar, in the Peshawar Museum.

The Peshawar Museum and Ashmolean figures both share a striking feature, a large hole in the top of the head. In the former, a spike still remains stuck in the hole. The same hole occurs in the famous little Indian ivory woman found in Pompeii, which was formerly thought to have been the holder or handle for some sacred symbol, or even a mirror. However, a recent study of this and another ivory figure of roughly the same date has shown convincingly that the figures were probably one of the legs of a low small table or stool, and this would also seem to have been the purpose of their metal counterparts. The fact that this free-standing figure incorporates a little plate below the feet supports the theory.

The Ashmolean bronze was hollow cast by the cire-perdue process. Badly rubbed as it now is, the detail must have been very fine. Although part of the clay core remains, the limits inherent in thermoluminescent dating are too wide for it to be of much use in dating fired clay of the historical period. What appears to be a tendency for the drapery of the skirt to flare outwards, noticeable in some sculptures in the north-west in the fourth and fifth centuries A.D., suggests a date at least in the 1st century of our era. There is a feeling of robust sensuality about this figure which is nearer to the sculpture of the late Sātavāhanas and the early Kuṣāṇas than to that of the last two centuries B.C.

METAL ANALYSIS
Nickel: 0.15; Iron: 0.35; Lead: 9.6; Tin: 14.6; and the remainder copper. No detectable traces were found of Zinc, Arsenic, Silver or Antimony.

PUBLISHED
J.C. Harle, "An Early Indian Bronze Figure", *From the East of Alexander's Empire*, Klaus Fischer Festschrift on the occasion of his 70th birthday, ed. J. Ozols and V. Thewalt, Köln (to appear).

10 COLOUR PLATE 3

Inscribed portion of the coping of a stone railing, spotted red sandstone. Mathura (?), first half of 1st century A.D.

Length $38\frac{1}{2}$ in. (97.8 cm.) Height 7 in. (17.8 cm.)
1983.24
Purchased with grants from the Eric North Bequest and the Friends of the Ashmolean.

Such railings were in common use in the earliest periods to demarcate a sacred enclosure, whether it contained a holy tree, the throne of a *yakṣa* or a *stūpa* (see nos.19 and 47). Since at least fifteen other portions of this coping are known, the railing to which it belonged probably enclosed a large monument such as a *stūpa*. Apart from the crisply carved frieze of some beauty, the Ashmolean example also bears, on the reverse side, an inscription of historical importance in its entirety. It reads: "Caused to be made by Kāśiputra Yaśaka, the confidant of King Sūryamitra, the son of Gopālī" (Härtel trans.).

The inscription provides evidence for the date and, less clearly, for the original location of the railing. Professor Härtel has argued, on epigraphical grounds as well as from the style of the carving, for the less well-documented of two kings named Sūryamitra, who reigned in Pañcāḷa, north-east of Mathura, in the first half of the 1st century A.D. The relatively small scale of the railing argues for an early date (see no.29) but the frieze, in spite of its leaping lions separated by palmettes which distantly echo older western Asian motifs, is in a style quite compatible with an early 1st century A.D. date. The railing may have stood in Ahicchattra, the principal site in Pañcāḷa, from which has come sculpture in the same style and distinctive stone as that of Mathura, and for which a sub-school of sculpture has been postulated; on the other hand, almost identically carved copings were excavated from the Kaṅkālī Ṭīlā site in Mathura. Of the other nine inscribed portions, only one so far known, in a private collection in Calcutta, bears the full text. Two others are in the National Museum, New Delhi, one in the Los Angeles County Museum of Art, and one in the Museum für Indische Kunst, West Berlin.

PUBLISHED
H. Härtel, "An Early Coping Stone Inscription from Mathura", *D.C. Sircar Memorial Volume*, ed, G. Bhattacharya, Calcutta, 1986.

11

Fragment of a small stele, with the upper portion of a goddess, red sandstone (with yellow flecks on reverse). Mathura, prob. 1st century A.D.

Height $5\frac{1}{4}$ in. (13.3 cm.)
O.S. 34
Purchased with a grant from the Max Müller Memorial Fund 1941.

Mathura, a city of great antiquity on the Jumna some 100 miles (161 km.) south of Delhi and a prolific centre of sculpture for centuries, was of immense importance during the Kuṣaṇa period (1st–3rd centuries A.D.) in the development of Indian sculpture. Its abundant remains have provided invaluable information about iconography, religious practices, holy places and shrines, Hindu and Buddhist as well as Jaina, at a crucial stage of their development.

While Mathura probably preceded Gandhara in producing images of the Buddha, its sculpture is probably best known for its exuberant representations of alluring women, both goddesses and the denizens of one or other of the several heavens, the latter often nearly life-size. This little fragment of a stele, on the other hand, undoubtedly represents one of the former, making as she does the gesture of *abhaya* ("do not fear") with her right hand. This hand has not been detached from the rest of the figure, the support behind it bearing cross-hatching to imitate a cushion and its fabric covering, a typical device in Kuṣāṇa Mathura. Also typical of these feminine figures is the way the hair is dressed, with a central pompom, a style almost certainly deriving ultimately from Rome.

The so-far unexplained arch or canopy enveloping the head on the relief occurs frequently in representations of goddesses in Mathura during the Kuṣāṇa period; but with the left hand missing, it is not possible even to guess at the exact identity of this little deity. The presence of a long trailing scarf as seen over her left shoulder suggests that she was standing.

Two features suggest an early date in the Kuṣāṇa period. One is that the hand in *abhaya* is turned slightly inward, the other is the joyous open expression of the face, unmarked by some of the stylistic mannerisms of the later Kuṣāṇa period (see nos. 12 & 14).

12

Head of a Tīrthaṅkara (or Jina), reddish sandstone. Probably Mathura, Kuṣāṇa period: 2nd–4th century A.D.

Height 6¾ in. (17.15 cm.)
1963.27
Gift of Mrs. Isa Cohn in memory of Dr. William Cohn

The absence of an *uṣṇiṣa* (see no.15) immediately distinguishes this head as having belonged to a statue of a Jina, one of the saviours of the Jain religion (see no.57), rather than the Buddha. The style and the nature of the stone indicate that Mathura or an associated site was the source of this sculpture, and indeed Mathura at this period produced greater numbers of Jina images than Buddhas. The heavy raised unbroken line indicating the eyebrows, the eyes with their peculiar treatment of the upper lids and the pouting lips all indicate a third or fourth century date, in the late Kuṣāṇa period. A smile is just beginning to steal across the lower part of the face, just as the eyes are becoming almond-shaped, precursors of the "spiritual" expression of Gupta Buddhas and Jinas. This and numberless other such figures, often quite crude in execution, may thus be considered in a sense transition pieces.

13

The Goddess Hārītī, relief plaque, spotted red sandstone. Mathura, 2nd–3rd century A.D.

Height 16¼ in. (41.3 cm.)
1971.36
Purchased with the aid of the Friends of the Ashmolean.

The folk origins of this goddess, associated with smallpox and hence "the stealer" (of children) are clear. Her cult must have been widespread amongst Buddhists, for she was frequently represented in the Kuṣāṇa period (first centuries A.D.) in both Gandhara, the present northernmost portions of Pakistan and parts of Afghanistan, as well as at Mathura. In both places she is usually shown seated, festooned with children and usually wearing a version of local dress. In Gandhara she is often accompanied by Kubera, also originally a folk deity (see no.18).

This figure of Hārītī is in the squatting position adopted by many figures during the Kuṣāṇa and Gupta periods at Mathura, from female goddesses to images of Sūrya, the Sun god (see no.26). She holds a large cup or bowl, tightly clasped by all five fingers, in her right hand; her left clasps a child. A small much worn figure at her feet appears to be the elephant-headed god, Gaṇeśa (see nos.43 and 52). If so, it is perhaps his earliest appearance, although his presence in this context is difficult to explain. The nature of the cross-barred frame into which the goddess has thrust her feet, although it occurs elsewhere, and with male figures as well, has not been explained. For the squatting pose, see no.25.

The "pompom" hair style (see no.11) is characteristic of Mathura during the Kuṣāṇa period. So is the architectural surround: the pillars with double capitals and the pediment in the shape of an ogee arch (*gavākṣa*). This last was to become one of the most ubiquitous of all Indian architectural motifs, reproduced a myriad times on Hindu and Jaina temples in subsequent centuries. The human figures in relief on the pillars, and even the figures with garlands in the beautiful Indian "flying" pose at the top corners (see also nos.32 & 41) all appear, appropriately, to be children. Relief stele such as this with an image of a god or goddess in the centre will now become the most common form of Indian sculpture.

14

Viṣṇu. (Upper portion of a small relief), mottled red sandstone. Mathura, Kuṣāṇa period, middle to third quarter of the 2nd century A.D.

Height 4 in. (10.2 cm.)
O.S. 38A

During the first centuries of the Christian era, most large sculptures from Mathura, both three-dimensional figures and those carved as reliefs on slabs, were either Buddhist or Jaina, reflecting perhaps not so much the dominance of these two faiths as the reluctance of the Hindus, for whatever reason is not known, to carve and worship large images in stone. Yet this period saw the emergence of the two great theistic faiths, with their supreme gods, Śiva and Viṣṇu, and their pantheons of lesser gods and goddesses (see no.11). Śiva appears to have been worshipped most often in the *liṅga* (see no.24), but anthropomorphic figures appear, usually small size reliefs, like this fragmentary image of Viṣṇu, identifiable by his club and the particular shape of his crown. He was

four-armed, the lower right hand making the gesture of "do not fear" (*abhaya*). The discus (*cakra*) most likely figured as another of Viṣṇu's weapons or symbols. He wears the *yajñopavīta*, the sacred thread traditionally worn by all Indian males of the three upper or twice-born castes.

Recent studies into the origins of Vaiṣṇavism, the great sectarian religion centring on Viṣṇu, tend to see in the earlier cult images such as this one, representations of Vāsudeva, one of five related folk heroes, rather than the solar deity of the most ancient sources. A similar and related folk origin is more precisely figured in the cowherd god Kṛṣṇa (see no.59). The style of this small Viṣṇu, with its exaggeratedly large eyelids, again suggests a date well into the Kuṣāṇa period. This has been confirmed by the finding of a practically identical sculpture in the carefully controlled excavations at Sonkh in a stratigraphical layer dated to the middle or third quarter of the 2nd century A.D.

15

Standing Buddha, grey schist. Gandhara, first centuries A.D.

Height $37\frac{1}{2}$ in. (95.3 cm.)
O.S. 26

Buddhism flourished in India for more than a thousand years after the Buddha's death (c.480 B.C.), and Buddhist monuments have survived from as early as the third and second century B.C., long before the first images of the Buddha were made. On reliefs he was represented, if at all, by symbols, his turban, his footprints, his begging bowl (see no.16). It was only in the first or second centuries A.D., probably due to doctrinal changes, that the first Buddhas were carved, in the round or in relief. This probably happened first at Mathura, but if so Gandhara followed shortly. Stylistically, however, the earliest Buddhas from Gandhara are worlds apart from those from Mathura. Whilst the latter are in an Indian idiom, Gandhara Buddhas, while predominantly Indian in iconography, reflect classical Graeco-Roman art to an extraordinary degree. An eminent authority has even gone so far as to see the art of Gandhara as a provincial Roman art in the service of Buddhism.

The Buddha's iconography is here fully developed. A large mole in the centre of his forehead, just above the nose, becomes known as one of the Buddha's characteristics. So does what appears to be a protuberance on the top of his head: the *uṣṇīṣa*, as it is called, is in reality a chignon or bun, a reminder that the Buddha came from the equivalent of the warrior caste, whose members did not cut their hair, wearing it in a bun under their turbans. The Buddha, however, has cast off his turban, as well as his jewellery. The extended ear-lobes, again, testify to his formerly having worn heavy ear-rings (see no.16). These features gave rise to one authority's dictum, that the Buddha is shown as a prince without ornaments and at the same time as a monk without a shaven head.

Since hundreds, if not thousands, of these images, were carved by the industrious stone carvers of Gandhara, the larger ones placed in the chapels of monasteries, it is thus easy to reconstitute the gestures of the missing hands: the right in the ritual gesture (*mudrā*) of *abhaya*, the left holding the folds of his *saṃghaṭī*. This is not the Roman toga, as was at one time assumed, but the upper garment of the Buddhist monk. Its plastic nature, however, with the folds of the garment lovingly treated for their own sake and completely masking the contours of the body, is totally in the Roman manner; equally classical is the treatment of the Buddha's head, ultimately based on that of the Greek Apollo.

The almond shaped eyes of this Buddha suggest a date a century or two later than that of the earliest Gandhara Buddhas, whose heads were more naturalistically treated and were often adorned with moustaches. The halo is of Middle Eastern origin.

16

Bodhisattva, grey schist, polished. From near Hoti Mardan, Gandhara, first centuries A.D.

Height 22 in. (56 cm.)
Given by Mrs. Gooding before 1914.
O.S. 24

Bodhisattvas, which play a part in Buddhist art second only to that of the Buddha himself, are future Buddhas who have chosen to remain on earth for the time being to help other creatures towards eventual Enlightenment. The Museum's example, a stele in very high relief, probably adorned the exterior of a *stūpa* (see no.19) or other religious edifice in a Buddhist monastery. As was the custom in Gandhara, the Bodhisattva is depicted dressed and bejewelled like a magnate of the region and the pose and iconography belong to the Indian tradition. The pose of the hands (*mudrā*) in this case signifies preaching (*dharmacakra-mudrā*), namely the Buddhist *dharma* or Law. As in the previous image, however, the style bears the clear mark of Graeco-Roman influence. The two narrow bands extending out from the turban almost certainly echo the ends of the knotted Greek diadem.

The figure sits on a low throne in the Indian pose known as *padmāsana*, both the feet placed, sole upward, on the thigh of the other leg. Below the cushion, against a background of drapery, two small figures in relief, with their hands in *añjali*, the gesture of respect or worship, flank what appears to be a begging bowl. That it is a sacred object is indicated by the throne on which it too is placed and it may stand for the Buddha (see no.15). The two worshippers, male and female, almost certainly represent the donors.

PUBLISHED
India and Greece, Connections and Parallels, Mārg Publications, ed. S. Doshi, Bombay, 1985, p.8, fig.4.

17

Birth of the Buddha, grey schist relief. Gandhara, probably Sikri, first centuries A.D.

Height $14\frac{1}{2}$ in. (36.8 cm.) Width $16\frac{1}{2}$ in. (41.9 cm.)
O.S. 3
Murray-Aynsley Collection.

Since the Buddha was a historical figure, incidents in his life, as in that of Christ, have always been a favourite with painters and sculptors. Of these, his birth numbers amongst the most important, along with his conception, his achievement of illumination under the Bodhi-tree at Bodhgaya, the first sermon preached in the deer park at Sarnath, the great miracle at Śrāvastī, and the *parinirvāṇa* or death, of which the Museum holds the companion piece to the birth.

Traditionally, the Buddha is shown being born from the right side of his mother, to be received by the god Indra. He wears a halo, as do the heads of several other male figures, all presumably Hindu gods. Their presence attests to their role in Buddhism: they are simply enlisted as particularly eminent worshippers of the Buddha.

Māyā, the Buddha's mother, is seen holding a frond of the highly stylised foliage canopy above her. This refers to the immemorial fertility association in India between a young girl and a tree, recorded in countless carvings (*śālabhañjikās*) where a young woman bends or clings to the foliage of a tree. On her proper left stands a young woman carrying a pot of consecrated water, essential at such an event, and probably a stick of sugar cane. The upward billowing curve of her scarf is a Western Asian and classical motif.

The attempt at illusionist carving and the treatment of the draperies all strongly suggest Roman reliefs of the first and second centuries A.D. The influence of the classical west is to a greater or lesser degree all-pervasive in Gandhara. At the same time the costumes and turbans are Indian, with the exception of Māyā's tunic-like upper garment, which is ethnically Kuṣāṇa.

PUBLISHED

J.C. Harle, *The Art and Architecture of the Indian Sub-Continent*, London, 1986, fig.58.

18

Pāñcika and Hārītī, grey schist. Gandhara, first centuries A.D.

Height $7\frac{1}{2}$ in. (19 cm.) Width $6\frac{3}{4}$ in. (17.1 cm.)
1962.42
Gift of Major P.C. Hailey

In this attractive sculpture, Pāñcika and Hārītī are seated together in a pose probably imitative of Roman tutelary couples. They are, in fact, Indian folk gods, he now dressed in a Kuṣāṇa tunic but with a Greek style cloak thrown over his shoulders, while Hārītī's dress is certainly non-Indian. Her crown in particular suggests a western origin. The cornucopia, with an animal's head at the base suggesting a rhyton (see no.5), is quite non-Indian. In fact, to pious Buddhists and caste Hindus alike, animal horn would have been anathema but they probably had no idea of the origin of the horn of plenty.

Pāñcika (sometimes conflated with Kubera) is associated with wealth. He holds a purse (part of his staff is missing) and coins are piled up below the throne. Hārītī, who is worshipped for the protection of children (see no.13) is here depicted as a goddess of plenty.

PUBLISHED

M. Hallade, *The Gandhara Style*, London, 1968, p.96 and pl.70.

19

Reliquary in the form of a *stūpa*, grey schist. Gandhara, 2nd–4th century A.D.

Height $4\frac{3}{4}$ in. (12 cm.)
1978.127
Purchased with the help of the Friends of the Ashmolean.

This small reliquary in the form of a *stūpa* underlines the earliest role of the *stūpa* as the repository of mortuary remains, in other words the *stūpa* as giant reliquary. An early text refers to *stūpas* being built over the widely distributed remains of the Buddha.

The *stūpa* is the monument *par excellence* of Buddhism and particularly the more primitive observance which flourishes to this day in Śri Laṅka, Burma and Thailand. In the first two countries, ancient *stūpas* whose foundations go back to the first millenium B.C. and reaching a diameter of 295 ft. (90 m.), still survive intact and are objects of great veneration.

The earliest *stūpa* to survive intact in approximately its original form is *Stūpa* II at Sañci, 2nd-1st century B.C. It has a low, less than hemispherical dome, surrounded, as an object of veneration, by a stone fence, one of the *vedikās* of which portions are illustrated in nos. 10 & 29. By the Kuṣāṇa period, the dome stands raised on a cylindrical element, as illustrated in the Museum's little reliquary. Examples of such *stūpas*, illustrated on countless reliefs, actually survive in Afghanistan and Swat (northern Pakistan). The shape of the square *harmikā* (the little railed platform on top of the dome) exactly reproduces the shape of this feature in the rare cases where it has survived; the stylised pyramid of parasols, only three in this relatively early example, is well known from stone reliefs and terracotta sealings depicting *stūpas*.

The contents of the *stūpa* consisted of two little gold boxes and one silver one, now empty.

20

Fragment of a frieze, grey schist. Gandhara, first centuries A.D.

Height 4 in. (10.2 cm.) Length 20 in. (50.8 cm.)
O.S. 4
Murray-Aynsley Collection.

To what extent Graeco-Roman motifs and architectural ornaments were borrowed in Gandhara is well illustrated by this frieze of *putti* holding up a garland, the principal decoration of hundreds of Roman sarcophagi. Close inspection will show that the head-dress (turbans?) of the *putti* and their heavy anklets are of Indian inspiration, as well as the flower that takes the place of the winged *putto* between the bird-figures, themselves a reversion to western classical types, more eagle than *haṃsa* (goose).

21

Attendant Figure, stucco. Gandhara, first centuries A.D.

Height $9\frac{3}{4}$ in. (24.8 cm.)
1970.154

Stucco, on a mud core, was used for sculpture at certain sites in Gandhara, as an alternative to stone. The technique was almost certainly imported from Alexandria. Not only Buddhas and Bodhisattvas, but also groups of figures, of which this fine example may have been a part, adorned the bases of *stūpas* at Jaulian and Mora Moradu, satellite monasteries of Taxila, near the present-day Pakistan capital of Islamabad. Entire chapels were occupied by sculpture in stucco or unbaked clay at Hadda, near Jalalabad, in Afghanistan.

The head of the figure illustrated is a noteworthy example of the skill in handling stucco achieved in Gandhara. Whereas most Gandhara Buddha heads, of which the Museum has several examples, verge on the insipid, the *morbidezza* with which this head is modelled gives it real poignancy. The identity of the figure is puzzling, however. A glance at the stone Bodhisattva (no.16) will show the same drapery and jewellery; on the other hand, the way in which the hair is treated, which is probably meant to indicate snail-curls, mounting to an *uṣṇīṣa* is only appropriate for a Buddha. The figure might conceivably be a *Buddha paré*, i.e. with jewellery and a crown, a common type in later periods; alternatively, the staff (?) held in one hand and the way the head is turned, suggest an attendant figure in a group, depicted without strict attention to iconographic norms.

22

Head of a bald man with moustache and beard, stucco, Gandhara, first centuries A.D.

Height $5\frac{7}{16}$ in. (13.9 cm.)
1958.2
Gift of Mr. E.M. Scratton

In almost all cases such detached heads once belonged to complete figures, sometimes in groups, more likely placed singly. This example, a "Socratic" type head of purely western classical inspiration, shows the ability of the sculptor in Gandhara to copy purely foreign types as a variant from the standardised heads of Buddhas and Bodhisattvas which were his stock in trade. To the contemporary Buddhist worshipper, versed to some extent in Brahmanical lore as he probably was, this personage was likely to represent a *ṛṣi* or sage. The heads, sometimes secured to the bodies with a wooden peg, were easy prey to vandals and spoliators but there is evidence that at times they simply dropped off. It can rain abundantly in Gandhara, obliterating the carving in the easily soluble stucco. A head in the Museum's collection shows where a fresh coating of stucco was applied, in which the features were modelled anew.

23

Lower portion of a male (?) figure, hollow cast bronze. Gandhara, first centuries A.D.

Height $4\frac{1}{2}$ in. (11.4 cm.)
O.S. 13A

This impressive though fragmentary little bronze, found in Gandhara but purely Graeco-Roman in style, was clearly an import. Such foreign works of art, dating from the 1st to 4th centuries A.D., have been found in considerable numbers in India and Pakistan, from the north-west to the northern Deccan, as well as in Afghanistan. Many of them can be traced to Alexandria. It is more difficult to determine the place of origin of this bronze, for the costume, marked by tassels at the back hanging down from an upper garment, is neither Greek, Roman nor Indian. It seems most likely to have been made in some Hellenistic milieu of Western Asia.

THE GUPTA PERIOD (A.D. 350–550)

24 COLOUR PLATE 4

Head of Śiva, spotted red sandstone.
Mathura, early 5th century A.D.

Height 12 in. (30.5 cm.)
O.S. 38
Purchased in 1939 with the help of Mr. and Mrs. H.N. Spalding and the National Art Collections Fund.

The Gupta period has been considered to be the Indian classical age in so far as, in Goetz's words, "it aspired to create a perfect, unsurpassable style of life". Its art, like that of 5th century Athens, influenced sculpture for many centuries and in lands far away from India. For the first time Indian sculpture was able to suggest higher spiritual states, a turning inward of the subject and an air of absorbed self-introspection. New too is an ability to combine the earthy and the dainty, a phrase of the same author.

Here the dainty treatment of Śiva's hair contrasts with the massive sculptural conception of the head as a whole; it is a head "outstanding in the elemental power, controlled and concentrated, that informs its every plane and curve. Severe and serene meditation is conveyed by half-open eyes, their gaze steadied by reverberating curves of lids and brows and the deep shadows between their intersecting planes. Correspondingly, the strands of hair that spread out like wings of a soaring bird clasp the vaulted forehead and frame the face . . . Abdicating all sensuality, the austere forehead and eyes are in command of the full-cheeked face. Compassion and detachment hover around the lips – now damaged and moustached. The third eye – symbolically the seat of the fire of destruction – extending across the entire height of the forehead, is here an essential part of Śiva's physiognomy. This head is indwelt by Śiva power; it is the god's true likeness."

Stella Kramrisch has done full justice to one of the most impressive of all the known images of Śiva, Mahādeva or the great god. He and Viṣṇu represent the twin pinnacles of the Hindu pantheon, each with its subordinate deities and demi-gods. Whether the head belonged to a full-length figure of the god or projected from a *mukha-liṅga*, the primordial phallic symbol of Śiva, has not been finally decided. It has even been suggested that it was part of a bust, although this is an almost unknown form of sculpture in India. Nor is it certain whether the moustache was part of the original conception; if so, it would point to an identification of the head with the fierce Aghora-bhairava, one of Śiva's emanations. The way in which the matted locks of the ascetic are portrayed here, as individual ringlets, would support such an identification, although there is also a suggestion of a certain kind of wig, one of the Gupta period's most urbane creations.

The stone is the spotted red sandstone of Mathura, and the style, with its unique blend of suavity and elemental plastic power, is unmistakably that of the Gupta period in its first full maturity.

PUBLISHED

S. Kramrisch, "Notes – A Śiva Head from Mathura," *Journal of the Indian Society of Oriental Art*, vol.VI (June–Dec. 1938), pp.200–202, pl.44; J.O. Woodward, *Treasures in Oxford*, London, 1951, pl.III; R.C. Majumdar and A.D. Pusalker, Eds., *The History and Culture of the Indian People*, vol.3, *The Classical Age*, Bombay, 1954, p.524, fig.38; J.C. Harle, "The Head of Śiva from Mathurā in the Ashmolean Museum – Is the Moustache Recut?" *Asian Review*, n.s., vol.2, no.1 (April 1965) p.38; J.C. Harle, *Gupta Sculpture*, Oxford, 1974, p.44, pl.50; S. Kramrisch, *Manifestations of Śiva*, Exhib. Cat., Philadelphia, 1981, p.15; G. Kreisel, *Die Śiva-Bildwerke der Mathurā-Kunst*, Stuttgart, 1986.

LITERATURE

J. Williams, *The Art of Gupta India*, Princeton, 1982.

25

Sūrya (the Sun-god) in the costume of a Kuṣāṇa prince, spotted red sandstone. Mathura, Gupta period, 5th century A.D.

Height $8\frac{5}{8}$ in. (21.9 cm.)
1972.45

The *udīcya* (northern) costume, featuring boots, a sort of tunic and a soft cap, its point tilted forward, first appears in Gandhara and Mathura around the first century of our era in depictions of the foreign people to whom the Kuṣāṇa rulers belonged. The squatting position makes a similar appearance at Mathura at this time, adopted by images of Sūrya, Hārītī (see no.13) and some little figures of mother-goddesses (*mātṛkās*).

The figure holds a small bowl (?), topped by a lotus blossom in his right hand; his left probably held a sword, of which only the bottom of the scabbard remains. Two little sitting lions, in profile on either side, recall the lion throne of some Kuṣāṇa princes or kings, whereas Sūrya is associated with the seven horses who draw his chariot, thus raising the question, as with some other images of the period, as to whether or not this is the Sun-god. Later, Sūrya is unmistakably identified by the presence of two attendants.

The sculpture is notable for its detail and the crispness of the carving. Whether the deeply cut lines around the sides and lower parts of the face outline a beard (some Kuṣāṇa kings are shown bearded on their coinage) or a faceguard, it is difficult to say.

PUBLISHED

J.C. Harle, *Gupta Sculpture*, Oxford, 1974, fig.51.; P. Pal, *The Ideal Image*, Exhib. Cat., Asia House, New York, 1978, no.5.

26

Relief of *makara*, terracotta. North India, probably Mathura region, c.400 A.D.

Height $7\frac{3}{4}$ in. (19.7 cm.) Length $16\frac{3}{8}$ in. (41.5 cm.)
Depth $3\frac{3}{8}$ in. (8.6 cm.)
1971.13

The *makara*, a half-aquatic monster, is perhaps the most frequently depicted fabulous animal in Indian art. This relief formed part of a frieze on one of the innumerable brick temples, of which only a handful have survived, built during and after the Gupta period in northern India. Not only were the niches filled with large, nearly life-sized reliefs of the principal deities, but the upper storeys were thronged with figures, some fanciful like this one, some even humorous, amidst the moulded brick architectural motifs.

Brio is one of the characteristics of the larger Gupta terracottas such as this one. Modelled with great freedom, the artist has managed to convey in clay the aquatic, almost slimy, texture of the beast's paws and snout; whereas the rear portion transforms itself, without the slightest awkwardness in the transition, into the great curling vegetal scrolls which are one of the glories of Gupta sculpture, both in stone and terracotta. The high relief and "lateral" cutting are one of the hallmarks of the style at its pinnacle.

PUBLISHED

J.C. Harle, *Gupta Sculpture*, Oxford, 1974, fig.148.; P. Pal, *The Ideal Image*, Exhib. Cat., Asia House, New York, 1978, no.33; ed. G. Michell, *In the Image of Man*, Exhib. Cat., Hayward Gallery, London, 1982, no.32.

THE POST-GUPTA PERIOD (A.D. 550–950)

27

Plaque or large tile with figures of ascetics(?), terracotta. Harwan, Kashmir, 4th–5th century A.D.

Height 20¾ in. (52.7 cm.) Width 13 in. (33 cm.)
1980.65
Purchased with the help of the Victoria and Albert Purchase Grant Fund and the E.H. North Bequest.

These large moulded tiles come from the courtyard surrounding the ruins of an apsidal-ended building at the Buddhist monastery of Harwan. Situated a few miles from Srinagar, it was unfortunately obliterated by a landslide some years ago. The tiles formed the risers of a bench at one end of the courtyard where presumably the monks sat. Similarly moulded but generally smaller tiles, bearing an astonishing variety of motifs, lined the floor of the courtyard. The Museum possesses some portions of these, one of which shows a mounted bowman.

The style of these and the other tiles, quite likely earlier than any other artefacts of the historical period from the Vale of Kashmir, is unique, combining Indian, Sassanian, possibly even Chinese motifs and some so far unknown elsewhere. The villainous faces of some of the figures above faintly recall Roman portrait sculptures. They are consequently particularly difficult to date. On the Indian time scale, they would appear to belong to the 4th–5th centuries A.D. Each plaque bears numerals in the Kharoṣṭhi script (here 32), probably indicating the position of each tile when they had been stamped on a large expanse of wet clay before being cut out, for firing, so that they could be re-assembled afterwards. An additional note of uncertainty is provided by the emaciated squatting figures in the two central panels, with their long hair. Buddhist practice did not encourage excessive fasting and Buddhist monks shaved their heads; perhaps these are spirits of the dead or ghosts (*pretas*), creatures of the burning-ground or charnel house which, set against the purity of the Buddhist monk or the Hindu ascetic desiring release from rebirth (*mumukṣā*), provide one of the constant themes of Indian religious art.

PUBLISHED
J.C. Harle, *Gupta Sculpture*, Oxford, 1974, p.57 and pl.144.

28

Two male heads, terracotta. Akhnur, Kashmir (Jammu), 5th–6th century A.D.

Right O.S. 50 – Height 3¼ in. (9 cm.)
Left O.S. 50A – Height 5 in. (12.7 cm.)
O.S. 50 and 50A
Purchased with the help of the Max Müller Memorial Fund.

These detached heads almost certainly belonged to figures adorning a *stūpa*, in the same way as the bases of *stūpas* in Gandhara, where terracotta was only rarely used, were often peopled with statues in stucco (see nos.21, 22). In style, with their sensitive and impressionist modelling, they are indeed very close to the late Gandhara stuccos from Haḍḍa. The relatively small number of early Kashmir terracottas, practically all from Akhnur, also show, along with a rather rococo sweetness, the same sharpness of characterisation which led André Malraux to see a Gothic quality in the Haḍḍa sculptures. The Ashmolean

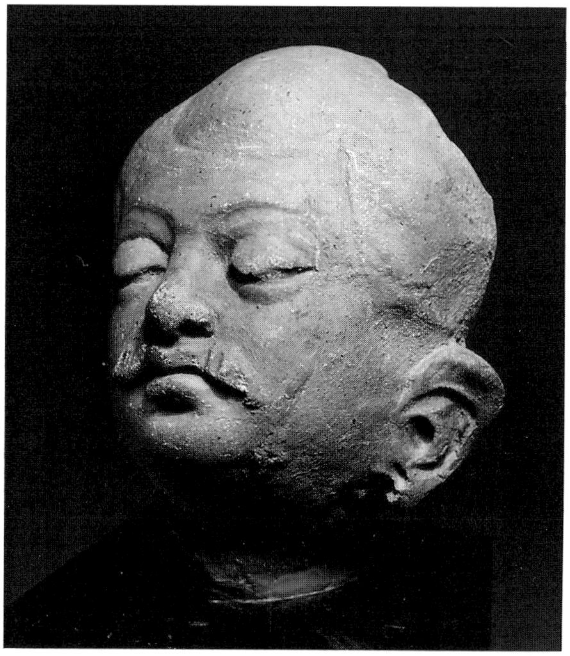

examples are particularly good examples of this feature: the rendering of apparent neurosis in the face of the man wearing a helmet, perhaps one of the soldiers in the army of Māra who sought to prevent the Buddha from achieving illumination at Bodhgaya, and of self-indulgent languor in the mustachioed head.

PUBLISHED

C.L. Fabri, "Akhnūr Terracottas", *Mārg*, VIII, 2, 1955, O.S. 50A illustrated fig.9B.

29

Portion of the coping of a stone railing, coarse-grained granite. Bodhgaya, 6th–7th century A.D.

Height 14 in. (35.6 cm.) Length 30 in. (76 cm.)
Width $11\frac{1}{2}$ in. (29 cm.)
X.391

Bodhgaya in Bihar, where, towards the end of the 6th century B.C., the Buddha, seated under a pīpal tree, achieved Illumination is probably the holiest of the places associated with the Buddha's life (see no.17). Over the exact spot now towers the Mahābodhi temple, but earlier shrines have stood there surrounded by the stone railings which in the early periods demarcated a sacred *enceinte* (see no.10). Portions of two railings remain, to the later of which the Ashmolean's coping belonged. It was probably archaic when it was carved, its erection probably due to the presence of the older (2nd–1st century B.C.) railing already there.

On one side runs a series of lotus or spiral roundels, separated by what may be highly conventionalised thunderbolts (*vajras*), on the other, a peacock, its tail, as often happens in the Gupta period, breaking out into swirls of foliage, precedes a *makara* (see no.26). A pair of geese faces in the opposite direction. All are favourites, throughout the ages, of classical Indian myth, literature and sculpture. The style is that of the late Gupta or early post-Gupta period.

LITERATURE

(Other portions of the coping): A.K. Coomaraswamy, *La sculpture de Bodhgāya*, *Ars Asiatica* XVIII, Paris, 1935, pls.III and XLI. Also Museum für Indische Kunst, West Berlin, IC8817, Sammlung Bastian 1879, pub. H. Härtel, *Indische Skulpturen*, Berlin, 1960, Tafel 31.

30

Head of a woman, red sandstone. Mathura, early 6th century A.D.

Height $6\frac{1}{4}$ in. (15.9 cm.)
1961.138
Gift of Penelope Chetwode

Only the head remains of what was once a complete female figure in very high relief, probably part of a group. The face with its almond-shaped eyes and fleshy lips has the sensual calm, combined with a certain hard-edged quality, of Mathura Buddhas of c.450 A.D. except that the gaze is not downcast, with the consequent exaggeration of the upper lid. The headdress, on the other hand, belongs to the very end of the Gupta period (c.320–550 A.D.) or even the outset of the post-Gupta, as does the right ear-ring, its "bar" already taking the form of a little baluster.

LITERATURE

See J.C. Harle, "A Gupta Ear-ring", *Senarat Paranavitana Commemoration Volume*, ed. L. Prematilleke, K. Indrapala and J.E. van Lohuizen-de Leeuw, Leiden, 1978, pp.78–80.

31

Durgā Mahiṣāsuramardinī, buff sandstone. Said to be from near Bharatpur, Rajasthan, c.700 A.D.

Height $10\frac{3}{4}$ in. (27.3 cm.)
O.S. 64

While still echoing the naturalism of the Gupta period, the more generalised forms of this fine, although much worn, little stele suggest a date c.700 A.D. The victorious goddess steps triumphantly on the head of the demon-buffalo, whose upraised rump, vigorously curved, suggests his now vanquished mighty power, while the way his left front leg is twisted back and the downturned mouth convey the pain and misery of his downfall. The goddess, pushing her trident into the animal's back with one of her hands, is perfectly balanced, as is the whole composition of the group.

The myth of Durgā (like Kālī, one of the terrible or combatant forms of the Goddess) killing Mahiṣa, an *asura* or demon in the form of a buffalo, is one of the most commonly represented in Indian art. The incident is first described in detail in the *Devī-Māhātmya*, a later addition to the *Mārkaṇḍeya-Purāṇa*. Mahiṣa was causing such terror and consternation amongst the gods that Śiva created a surrogate, Durgā, to slay the monster, each of the gods bestowing upon her their several powers, symbolised iconographically by their weapons. The trident, for instance, is Śiva's weapon *par excellence*.

Along with small figures of Vāsudeva (see no.14), little stele figuring Durgā killing the buffalo, also of small size, like no. O.S. 77 in the Museum's collection, all carved in Mathura during the Kuṣāṇa period, are the first Hindu images to be made in large numbers. In these early images, the goddess stands, usually straight-legged, behind the buffalo, with one stiff right arm pressing down on his back which he rears up, with his head pressed against the goddess's left shoulder. Then, probably at some time in the 5th century, this iconographic formula is drastically altered. The position of the buffalo is reversed (as here), with his head held down by Durgā's right foot and his rump raised on her left side. This arrangement prevails henceforth in northern India and parts of the Deccan.

LITERATURE

See O. Viennot, "The Mahiṣāsuramardinī from Siddhi-ki-Guphā at Deogarh", *Journal of the Indian Society of Oriental Art*, n.s. IV (1971–72), note 27.

This splendid circular composition of eight male figures, their legs interlocked and radiating out like the spokes of a wheel, is in the finest early post-Gupta (c.A.D. 550–950) style, with a rhythm and a liveliness which is characteristic at this time of the carving of ceiling slabs and figures on door lintels rather than of full length images of the gods. Note the quality of the carving and the precision, to within millimetres, of the placing of the interlocking legs and feet.

Carved ceiling slabs are a feature of temples in the Deccan and northern India after the Gupta period. At this time they bear relatively simple compositions of gods and demi-gods; in later times they become almost incredibly intricate, with scores of figures in increasingly abstract patterns, but the sculptural qualities much diminished. The circular shape and relatively small size of this slab suggest it once belonged to the porch of a small temple; alternatively it may have adorned one portion of a coffered ceiling in the hall of a larger shrine.

Each figure holds a sword, and there are indications of clouds (or flames?) in very low relief on the ground. These are not sufficient clues to enable the eight figures to be identified. Being eight in number suggests

32 COLOUR PLATE 5

Ceiling slab with eight armed men, red sandstone. Northern Gujarat or southern Rajasthan, c.750 A.D.

Diameter 30 in. (76 cm.)
1985.5
Purchased with the help of the Victoria and Albert Purchase Grant Fund and the E.H. North Bequest.

the *aṣṭadikpālas* or guardians of the eight directional quarters, but by this time these have individual identities. The *aṣṭamūrtis* related to the different elements (fire, air, water, etc.) seem more likely candidates in view of the relief carving on the ground.

One authority, however, has suggested that these figures, in what is essentially the "flying" pose, might be *vidyādharas*, magicians and semi-divine creatures of the air. They do not, as a rule carry anything but wreaths or garlands. The name means literally "bearers of magical powers". Viṣṇu's sword is named Vidyā on occasion and the ceiling slab could, in a Viṣṇu temple, be a meaningful and appropriate semi-verbal, semi-visual pun. Another possibility is that eight Vasus, creatures of the elements, are represented here.

An engraving of a roughly similar slab was published by Burgess and Cousens as being one of two in a small ruined temple at Vaḍnagar. It shows sixteen men holding swords similarly grouped, although the legs, partly due to the increased number, are more awkwardly arranged. The number sixteen does not immediately suggest a group of deities. From its style the slab appears to be of a later date.

LITERATURE

See J. Burgess and H. Cousens, *The Architectural Antiquities of Northern Gujarat*, London, 1903, pl.58, 2.

33 COLOUR PLATE 6

Lokeśvara-Padmapāṇi, brass. Attributed to the Punjab, 6th–8th century A.D.

Height 6¼ in. (15.9 cm.)
1971.14
Purchased with the help of the late Mrs. Pamela B. Knight.

This notable metal sculpture is here attributed, with some temerity, to the Punjab, meaning the plains north-west of Delhi watered by the five great rivers (*Panj-āb*: five waters or rivers) tributary to the Indus. No metal images of the period have yet been found there, but the attribution seems reasonable in view of the figure's many iconographic and stylistic affinities to numerous images from Kashmir and the Swat valley, including graffiti on boulders in the latter region, combined with a suavity of modelling which seem to relate it more closely to Gupta and early post-Gupta sculpture in metropolitan India.

The iconographic formula, with the Bodhisattva seated on a wicker stool or toffet, upon which one leg is drawn up and laid flat (*lalitāsana*), his right elbow leaning on the upper part of the leg while the hand points to the slightly inclined head, harks back to the art of Gandhara. There, relief figures of Bodhisattvas, always subsidiary figures, frequently appear in this pose, usually with the index finger of the right hand actually touching the head. So far this pose has not found a corresponding description in the texts, but its undoubtedly pensive, and perhaps sorrowing, mood may indeed indicate the Bodhisattva as *mahākāruṇika* ("Lord of great compassion"). More generally, the two-armed figure, with the left hand holding a long-stemmed lotus, can be identified as Lokeśvara, another name for Avalokiteśvara, or Padmapāṇi, "he who holds a lotus".

Several images, notably the splendid one in Asia House, New York (Mr. and Mrs. John D. Rockefeller 3rd collection), include all these essential features, as well as the sacred thread and the animal skin over the left shoulder, and are indisputably from Kashmir or Swat. They usually display, however, a small figure of a meditation Buddha in the head-dress (see no. 38), missing here. The shape of the petals of the beautiful double lotus band atop the stool in the Ashmolean figures is pure Kashmiri and so is the rather dropsical outline of the left leg. But the plastic quality is quite different, closer to early post-Gupta norms in its suavity, compared to the often slap-dash modelling of Kashmiri bronzes and their almost buttery quality, due in part to the high proportion of lead in their composition. The smooth torso of the Ashmolean's figure totally lacks the rather ostentatious chest muscles of most Kashmiri sculptures. Lead is notably absent (see below), replaced by a large admixture of zinc, turning the alloy into brass, which results in a feeling of hard precision.

Two other features distinguish this Padmapāṇi Lokeśvara from Kashmiri figures. One is the way in which the hair, apparently gathered into a ring at the top, cascades down in a series of wire-like volutes on one side of the head, and drops down in two large loops on the left, a combination not seen elsewhere. The other is that the pelt on the shoulder has a lion rather than a deer head. This again suggests post-Gupta India, where Śiva, associated with the lion-skin, tends to share iconographical details with Avalokiteśvara.

This image, like many other metal sculptures from

the north-west of the Indian sub-continent, came out of Tibet in recent years, where it had most likely been for centuries.

METAL ANALYSIS

Copper: 71%; Zinc: 27%; Tin: 2%. Only small amounts of other metals were found, and no lead.

PUBLISHED

J.C. Harle, "An Early Brass Image of a Bodhisattva with Kashmiri or Swat Valley Affinities", *South Asian Archaeology*, 1975, Leiden, 1979, pp.126–34.

LITERATURE

P. Pal, *Bronzes of Kashmir*, Graz, 1975.

34
Sūrya, bronze with silver and gold inlay. Kashmir, 7th–8th century A.D.

Height $7\frac{7}{8}$ in. (19.8 cm.)
1986.2
Gift of Douglas and Mary Barrett

This slightly unusual bronze figure of Sūrya, the Sun god (see no.25), probably dates from as early as the end of the 7th century. Except for his boots, there are no specifically Kuṣāṇa traits to his costume: his crown, the way his hair is dressed, and the scarf looped down between his two arms with fluttery ends, are all reminiscent of certain generally small reliefs in potstone, found in north-west India and probably of late Gupta or early post-Gupta date; the Museum has one such fragment (X.244). So is the shape of the little cape or bolero over the god's shoulders, perhaps a distant echo of the Greek schlamys.

The principal figure holds a highly stylised lotus in each hand. A massive sword hangs by his left side, in contrast to the small dirk suspended horizontally below the belt on many Kashmiri male Hindu gods. The two attendants are called Piṅgala, who may well hold, as prescribed, a pen in one hand and an ink-pot in the other, and Daṇḍā who, as his name implies, holds a staff (*daṇḍa*). They too wear boots and, instead of the Kuṣāṇa square cut tunic or a coat, the same long gown, slit at the sides, as Sūrya. The eyes of all the figures are inlaid in silver and there is a small inlaid gold dot in the middle of Sūrya's forehead.

METAL ANALYSIS

Iron: trace; Copper: 91.0; Lead: 1.2; Tin: 7.6; Antimony 0.18.

35
Terracottas. Khotan, Central Asia; 5th–6th century A.D.

Measurements: $1\frac{1}{2}$ in. (3.8 cm.) to $3\frac{1}{2}$ in. (8.8 cm.)
Gift of Dr. A.F. Rudolph Hoernle, 1903
X.1, 12, 21, 38, 41, 66, 67, 68

Khotan, near the southern edge of the great Takla Makan desert, is in Central Asia. A few of the objects from Khotan and nearby sites such as Dandan Uilig and Yotkan, in the Museum's collection have been included here for a number of reasons. Khotan is the nearest to India of the Central Asian sites brought to light by the great European explorers of the turn of the century; the expeditions to Khotan were mounted in India and Sir Aurel Stein, a Hungarian by birth but a naturalised Briton who made his career in India (and Central Asia) was Britain's champion in the "Great Game" of Central Asian exploration and pioneer archaeology, along with the Swede Sven Hedin, the Russian Klementz, the German von le Coq and the Frenchman Pelliot. A much older connection, moreover, links Khotanese artefacts with India: the terracottas in particular are largely of Indian inspiration when they do not derive in part, as does some of Indian art itself, from Hellenistic and Roman examples. Khotanese artefacts, moreover, are not found in many museums, perhaps a half dozen in the world. Finally, most of the Khotanese objects in the Ashmolean, some one hundred and thirty, were the gift of Dr. A.F. Rudolph Hoernle, one-time Government Epigraphist for India, selected from his much larger collection given to the British Museum, all of which pre-date the Stein expeditions. This is

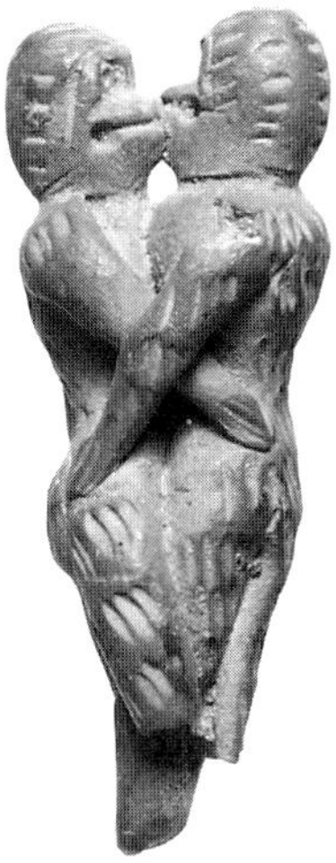

succinctly stated, as also how they first passed into European hands, in an unpublished letter dated Oxford, 1 March 1904, to A.J. (later Sir Arthur) Evans, the excavator of Knossos and at the time Keeper of the Ashmolean Museum. Hoernle's collection was acquired, on his instructions, by the British Agents in Kashgar, Leh and other outposts, on behalf of the British Government in India and sent to him in Calcutta where he was stationed. Some of the terracottas still bear the marking "M" and a number in ink, referring to a particular package sent by McCartney, the best known of these men. It was upon realising the approximate source of such material that Stein mounted his first expedition.

These terracottas, some in the round and none more than 3 inches or 7.6 cm. in their largest dimension (nos. 1 and 12 are less than half that) are all marked by their spontaneity of modelling and a vivid sense of the droll. This includes the appliqué lion masks, detached from some long-smashed pot. From Iran to China, at this period, appliqué decoration was extremely popular, much of it, like nos. X66, 67 and 68, ultimately of Western classical inspiration. An exception is no. 36b below.

PUBLISHED

R.F. Rudolph Hoernle, "A Report on the British Collection of Antiquities from Central Asia", *Journal of the Royal Asiatic Society of Bengal*, XVIII, extra no. 1 (1899) and LXX, extra no. 1 (1901). See also Sir Aurel Stein, *Ancient Khotan*, Oxford, 1907; Roderick Whitfield, *The Art of Central Asia: the Stein Collection in the British Museum*, Tokyo, 1982.

36

a) Bodhisattva, stucco. Khotan, 5th–6th century A.D.

Height 6 in. (15.2 cm.)
X.81, 83
Gift of Dr. A.F. Rudolph Hoernle, 1903

b) Appliqué medallion, terracotta, stamped or moulded. Khotan, 5th–6th century A.D.

Diameter $2\frac{1}{2}$ in. (6.4 cm.)
1984.26
Gift of Mrs. Alethea Pitt; collected by her father, Sir Armine Dew, K.C.I.E., C.S.I.

The painted relief of a Bodhisattva(?), probably moulded, formed part of the decoration of a wooden doorway. It is a composition of considerable elegance and characteristic of the achievements in alternative materials in a region where stone, and certainly any tradition of working in stone, appear to have been non-existent.

The appliqué medallion, with its pearl border, was part of a large pot, of which there is an intact example in the Museum für Indische Kunst, West Berlin, similarly decorated with round medallions surrounded by a pearl band, but where the motifs in its medallions are of Indian or classical inspiration, as are the appliqué lion masks of no. 35, the bearded figure in the Museum's example shows stylistic affinities to art further east. In particular, the hooked eyebrows are reminiscent of the famous wall painting of Mahākāśyapa from Kyzil.

This and several other small terracottas from Khotan were acquired by Sir Armine Dew in the North West Frontier Province in the 1920s.

37

Bust of a man with a water-skin and a stringed instrument, terracotta. Khotan, Central Asia, probably Yotkan; 5th–6th century A.D.

Height (including modern moulded base) $3\frac{13}{16}$ in. (9.6 cm.)
Width (at elbow) 3 in. (7.6 cm.)
1958.116
F.A. Andrews Bequest; collected by Sir Aurel Stein.

This is perhaps the most lively of the terracotta finds by Sir Aurel Stein in Khotan, and one of the few figurines. The light colour is characteristic of the terracottas from Yotkan, and so is the technique of the lightly incised eyes, but the bearded face is conceived fully in the round. Most of the detached heads found at Yotkan on the other hand are doll-like and flattened. The figurine illustrated here lends some credence to the judgement of a contemporary that the Khotanese, as well as being frivolous, were exceptionally fond of music.

38
Head of Avalokiteśvara, stone. Probably from Bodhgaya, c.750 A.D.

Height 9½ in. (24.1 cm.)
O.S. 61

This head of the Bodhisattva Avalokiṭésvara is here identified by the little figure in the headdress, seated in *padmāsana* (where one folded leg is placed on top of another) and with hands laid in his lap, palm upwards (*dhyāna-mudrā*), the gesture signifying meditation. This is quite proper since the figure represents one of the five meditation Buddhas. These are not "historical" Buddhas, such as the Buddhas whose lives paralleled that of Śakyamuni in previous aeons (*kalpas*), but purely intellectual creations standing for metaphysical concepts. They appear once or twice in the headdress of Gandhara Bodhisattvas, evidence that the great changes in doctrine had commenced, whereby the simple tenets of early Buddhism eventually yielded to the complex construction of what came to be known as the Mahāyāna or Great Vehicle, culminating in the massed pantheons and magical practices of Tibet.

The Bodhisattva wears a *jaṭāmukuṭa*, a headdress or crown in which the jewelled portions terminate in the interwoven matted locks of the ascetic. It is particularly appropriate to Śiva, with whom Avalokiteśvara shares some iconographic features. The treatment of the neck, with its concentric ribs of fat, was widely adopted as a feature of god-like power and beauty. The exaggeratedly fleshy lips and eyebrows arching high over the eyes are regional stylistic traits which become more marked with the beginning of the Pāla period (c.A.D. 750) in eastern India. For later examples of the Pāla style, see nos.42, 43, 46 and, of the Pāla-Sena style, no.48.

39
Wrestlers, black stone, the base built up with plaster. Eastern India, 7th–8th century A.D.

Height 16 in. (40.6 cm.) Width 9½ in. (24.1 cm.)
Thickness 13½ in. (34.3 cm.)
O.S. 52

The fluting which can be discerned at the top of this fragment identify it as part of a pillar and not neces-

sarily the base, since, from the 6th century onwards, temple pillars were interrupted with median bands which were often richly decorated. Semi-circular medallions such as this one with a pearl border and bearing relief figures, accompanied by foliage work usually incorporating a *kīrtimukha* (see below) are, moreover, found on a great many of the pillars which have survived from temples of the post-Gupta period all the way from Bodhgaya to Mahasthan in Bangladesh.

The grotesque mask (*kīrtimukha* or "face of glory"), part human, part leonine and even with a suggestion of horns, has its remote origins in western classical antiquity (see no. 35). In later times it tends to lose its human features, and the fact that this *kīrtimukha* is still recognizably human argues for a relatively early date for the fragment, in the 8th and possibly even the late 7th century A.D. As for the wrestlers, wrestling has always been popular in the northern part of India and representations on reliefs show a knowledge of the sport. Where other indications exist, the contestants have been variously identified as those heroes from myth or the epics who engaged in wrestling contests, such as Bhīma and Jarasandha, or Kṛṣṇa and Cāṇūra, but here there are not sufficient clues to suggest an identification.

PUBLISHED

W. Cohn, "Der Wettkampf im Ringer, ein Relief im Museum of Eastern Art, Oxford", *Schriften des Museums Rietberg, Zürich*, no. 2, pp. 65–71.

LATER HINDU, BUDDHIST AND JAIN SCULPTURE

40

Varāha, the great Boar, dark brownish-grey stone. Northern Madhya Pradesh or Bihar, 9th–10th century A.D.

Height 33 in. (83.8 cm.) Length 24 in. (61 cm.)
1969.43

The myth of Viṣṇu, in his incarnation as a boar (Varāha), rescuing the goddess Earth (Bhū Devī) from the primeval waters, strange as it may seem at first to non-Indians, has always been one of the most popular of creation myths. Images of the god in human form but with a boar's head begin to appear at Mathura in Kuṣāṇa times. This tradition culminated in the great Boar panel of the early Gupta period at Udayagiri (Vidiśā) but continued thereafter to be a popular feature of the Vaiṣṇava iconographic repertory in most parts of India.

The less familiar type of image, where the god is depicted in purely animal form, is first seen at Eran, in western Madhya Pradesh, in gigantic form; thereafter it enjoyed a considerable vogue, but one largely limited to Madhya Pradesh and Bihar. While lacking the exultant power of the man-boar images, with one leg bent at the knee propelling him upwards and the Earth hanging to a tusk or nestling in the crook of his arm, these all-animal sculptures are treasure-houses of Indian iconography, set off by details of a charming whimsicality.

At least half the surface of the boar's body is covered with low-relief figures, either single or massed in long bands. Some of these can be identified as the *ṛṣis* or sages, who, according to the myth, saved themselves by clinging to the bristles of the mythical Boar. There are animals, ritual objects and Vaiṣṇava symbols. Single figures are dotted around on the boar's head, his legs and even in his ears. Under his feet are the *śaṅkha* (conch) and the *cakra* (discus) and on the other side, where Bhū Devī stands, her head beside one of the boar's tusks, lies the *gadā* (mace), one of Viṣṇu's principal symbols. The two personified treasures (*padmanidhi* and *śaṅkhanidi*) are set below the boar's belly, whereas Brahmā sits beside the *cakra*, with a devotee drinking from his long sacrificial spoon.

A large *nāginī* or serpent-goddess, identified by a hood of multiple serpent heads, fronts the image; she rises from a tortoise. Both belong to the imagery of the waters, the tortoise having been used as fulcrum or pestle when the Milk Ocean was churned, another creation myth.

The jar of *amṛta*, the liquor of immortality, lashed to the boar's tail by a complicated knot, the fanciful little cap and the little ropes knotted around its ankles, are all odd touches of whimsy lightening the rather overburdened iconography and heavy form of this image. No explanation has yet been found for the stump rising up behind the boar's head, a feature of all these images.

PUBLISHED

In the Image of Man, ed. G. Michell, Exhib. Cat., London, 1982, p.202.

41

Standing Brahmā (?), brown stone. Madhya Pradesh or northern India, 10th–11th century A.D.

Height 17 in. (43.2 cm.)
O.S. 62

This small stele shows the god Brahmā standing in *abhaṅga* (or *samapada*), a pose in which neither leg is bent and consequently no flexion is imparted to the body. Behind him is a *haṃsa* (goose). The little figure with his hands in the gesture of respect or salutation (*añjali*) is presumably a devotee and possibly the donor. The two small figures on either side at the top in the flying position are iconographic markers, like the parasol in other instances; celestial creatures of no individuality, they simply reflect the divine stature of the god and the respect due to him. Their hands are also in *añjali*.

The god is three-headed; the hair of the central head is arranged in three tufts (*triśikhā*). In his upper hands he holds a staff and, almost certainly, the long narrow rectangle of a palm-leaf manuscript (*pustaka*). Unfortunately the lower hands are damaged or missing. This is particularly unfortunate since the identification of this image is uncertain because of iconographic ambiguities and contradictions, and it has been suggested that it represents Skanda (Kārttikeya), the son of Śiva. Skanda's vehicle is a peacock, which the bird portrayed here might well be and, as a young prince (Kumāra), he is often shown as *triśikhin*. On the other hand, his multiple heads, when shown, number six, having been nurtured by six mothers. The book moreover, as symbolising the Vedas, is not one of his attributes, whereas it is definitely associated with Brahmā, who is himself usually depicted with three heads.

The slight iconographic uncertainty attending this image may be due to the fact that while Brahmā had a commanding position in the Vedas, the sacred hymns composed c.1250 B.C. upon which the early Brahmanical religion was based, and, as the Creator, is still considered a member of the traditional Hindu trinity of Brahmā, Viṣṇu and Śiva, most of his attributes were usurped in time by the other two divinities and he never became the object of a cult. Temples dedicated to Brahmā in India are so rare as to be virtually non-existent.

42

A form of Devī (the Goddess), bronze. Eastern India, c.900 A.D.

Height 6 in. (15.2 cm.)
O.S. 104

The Pāla period (750–1150 A.D.), particularly in its

earlier phase, was a golden age of bronze casting in Northern India. Some of the bronzes are amongst the most elaborate ever cast on the Indian Subcontinent and these small figurines (see also no.45) give little indication of the intricate and multi-figured compositions of the more important bronzes. Nonetheless, the modelling of the feminine deity here is of the highest standard and the whole image is attractive in its proportions and the spacing and arrangement of the elements of what is, considering its small size, a remarkably rich iconography.

The goddess stands, her weight evenly borne by each leg, on a lotus base. Her upper right hand holds an *akṣa-mālā*, her upper left an unusual attribute: either fire (*agni*), a triple rod (*tridaṇḍa*) or a trident carved out of wood. Her lower right hand makes the *varada* or boon-giving gesture, possibly holding a fruit as well. The lower left hand holds a spouted jar. On the surround (proper left) is a miniature *liṅga* with its *pīṭha* (base); opposite, on the other side, is a tiny image of Gaṇeśa, the elephant-headed god, the son of Śiva and Pārvatī. On top of the pedestal stand two banana plants or plantains (*raṃbhā*) on either side, with a lion (Pārvatī's vehicle) and a horned animal, both couchant and facing a little conical object, probably representing a pillar of fire. Climbing on to the base is an iguana (*godhā*).

There is some doubt about the identity of this image. Most of her symbols or attributes here leave no doubt that she belongs to the pantheon associated with Śiva, that she is, in fact, a form of the Goddess, Devī. Others are unusual and highly distinctive, such as the plantain, the iguana and the pillar of fire. There are, moreover, corresponding large images in stone from the same Pāla period, as well as other small bronzes, all of which have been identified as Rambhā, from a reference in the *Agni Purāna* (De Mallmann, pp.139–40). Recently, however, another authority has claimed that this identification rests on a mistranslation. The difficulty in making a firm identification comes in part from the looseness of the language of so many of the traditional texts, and the lack of absolute consistency, with such a rich iconography, amongst the images of this type. Other identities proposed for this figure are Gaurī, Maṅgalachaṇḍī and Siddhā.

PUBLISHED

G. Bhattachaya, "A Special Type of Devī figure from Bihar and Bengal", *Facets of Indian Art*, ed. R. Skelton, A. Topsfield, S. Stronge and R. Crill, London 1986.

LITERATURE

M.-T. de Mallmann, *Les Enseignements Iconographiques de l'Agni Purāṇa*, Paris, 1963; C. Picron, "De Rambhā à Lalitadevī dans la Statuaire Pāla-Sena en Pierre", *Artibus Asiae*, 42, 4 (1980), pp.282–302; S. Mukhopadhyay, *Caṇḍī in Art and Iconography*, Delhi, 1984, p.122.

43
Gaṇeśa, bronze. Eastern India, 9th–10th century A.D.

Height 5 in. (12.7 cm.)
X.182

Gaṇeśa, the elephant-headed god, is four-armed and seated in a relaxed position (*lalitāsana*), one leg drawn up on his lotus pedestal, the other hanging down as much as the god's excessive chubbiness will permit. His vehicle, variously described as a rat, mouse or shrew, near his right foot, gazes up at him. As in no.52, the god's crown appears to be interwoven with his long locks of hair(?) into a *jaṭā-mukuṭa*. In his lower

right hand he holds the broken end of his right tusk, in his left is the bowl from which Gaṇeśa, as in almost all images of this god, is picking some little round cakes with his trunk. His left rear hand holds the axe (*paraśu*), the right what is probably a radish (*mūlaka*), with a little hooded serpent head beside it.

Below the circular lotus pedestal is a stepped, four-legged throne and there is a drop-shaped bezel for a jewel near the apex of the *prabhāvali*.

44
Viṣṇu in the Lotus, bronze. Eastern India or Nepal, 11th–12th century

Height 5 in. (12.7 cm.)
X.285
Gift of Mrs. Hoey

In Indian art, the lotus (*nymphea pubescens* and *nymphea stellata*) is by far the most frequently represented of all the rich flora of the sub-continent. Flower, petal, seed-pod, bud or leaf are omnipresent from earliest times; they serve as emblems, stands, seats or thrones, as well as petalled mouldings. Yet, as is often the case in India, it is difficult to define the symbolism of the lotus in a single formula. The lotus's rise from the waters (and mud), spotless and unwettable, into the realm of air and light, is consonant with much aquatic and cosmological symbolism, including creation myths (see no.40). The lotus is also equated with spiritual insight (*bodhi*), residing in the heart (*hṛdaya*). Like the heart it expands in the light of knowledge

or devotion. According to Tantric interpretation (a relatively late and esoteric manifestation of Indian religion, with a highly mystical and even magical metaphysic), an image of the deity in a lotus, i.e. the heart, indicates the supreme self-identification of the individual consciousness with God.

The petals of this bronze sculpture are hinged, thus permitting the lotus to open and close. Inside sits a four-armed Viṣṇu in *padmāsana*, on what one authority has called the seed-pod of the lotus. He holds a lotus in his right upper hand, a conch in the left and a sweet lime (or *mātuluṅga*) in his left front hand; the object in his front right hand cannot be identified. Of eight petals, seven have survived. On their insides, separately cast, are attached little figures of incarnations (*avatāras*) of Viṣṇu. Some, like Varāha, Narasiṁha and Bālarāma belong to the standard group of eight. Others, including probably Dattatreya, are difficult to identify. They are in most cases two-armed and only hold a single symbol, a bow, an arrow or flute, or a club. They may represent major incarnations (e.g. Rāmacandra or Kṛṣṇa) or else perhaps minor ones, of which there are a great number.

A number of bronze lotuses of eastern Indian origin are known, usually on stems and with similarly movable petals. The central figure, instead of Viṣṇu, is usually a divinity of the Buddhist Mahāyāna or even the Tantric pantheon. Such an ambiance may account for the *avatāras* of the Museum's lotus not corresponding to the usual representations of the group. There are Newāri numberings on the base and the petals, suggesting a Nepali origin for this piece which is particularly notable for the fineness of its casting.

PUBLISHED

S. Kramrisch, *The Art of Nepal*, Exhib. Cat., New York, 1964, no.14.

45

Umāmaheśvara, brown sandstone. Madhya Pradesh, early 11th century

Height 23 in. (58.4 cm.)
O.S. 70
Presented by Sir S.M. Tagore

This is probably the archetypal icon of the later Hindu period in North India and parts of the Deccan. Śiva (Maheśvara, the "great god") sits in *lalitāsana* (the same pose as in nos.33 and 58), with Umā (another name for Pārvatī, Śiva's *śakti* or divine Power), seated on his left thigh, her right arm thrown around the neck of the god; in the other hand she holds a mirror.

Śiva, with his unusually tall *jaṭā-mukuṭa* (the crown entwined with the matted hair of the ascetic and

adorned with the crescent moon), is four-armed. His two upper hands hold the trident and a tricephalous serpent, his lower left clasps Umā around the waist, while his lower right in *vyākhyāna-mudrā*, the gesture signifying spiritual instruction, is placed near her right breast. Below are the usual assemblage: Śiva's offspring, Gaṇeśa and Skanda (Kārttikeya), the latter barely indicated by a crude little peacock's head, Nandī the bull and Bhṛṅgi, the skeletal ascetic, in a dancing pose. The lion, rarely represented in this icon, is Umā's vehicle.

Above, under a pair of flying celestial beings bearing garlands, sit two deities, whose emblems and implements are difficult to discern, but they most likely are Brahmā, because of his paunch, on the proper right, and Viṣṇu on the left.

46

COLOUR PLATE 7

Standing Buddha, stone. Probably Bodhgaya, 10th–11th century

Height 3 ft $8\frac{1}{2}$ in. (112 cm.)
O.S. 56

This fine stele attests to the enduring vitality of the Gupta style which created Buddhas of this type some

six hundred years earlier. At the same time it is an easily recognizable product of the Pāla period. Typical is the surround, a pearl wreath bordered by an interlocked flame design. The leaves of the highly stylised tree behind the Buddha do not have the characteristic shape of the leaves of the pipal tree; yet it has a weird botanical similitude.

Marvellously projected against the otherwise plain ground, the Buddha stands with considerable *déhanchement*. His lower garment, commencing just below the navel, causes a slight swelling of the abdomen above; it extends below the upper garment in a similar and exactly parallel double pleat. The upper garment, likewise wholly transparent, ends in a transverse wavy line resembling the *yajñopavīta*, the sacred thread traditionally worn by the three twice-born castes. The right hand (missing) was almost certainly in *abhaya*, the "do not fear" gesture. The left holds, gathered-up, the ends of the upper garment. There are three rings or folds around the Buddha's neck and he is depicted as usual at this time with the *ūrṇā*, his hair in little ringlets or snail curls, with the *uṣṇīṣa*.

All the features of this Buddha, except for the curious way the top of the upper garment is treated, derive from or are slight modifications of the formula first devised at Sarnath in the second half of the 5th century. The *déhanchement* is more pronounced, there is no attempt to indicate the presence of the sexual organs and the face is a narrower oval but the smooth interlocking volumes of the body, although more sharply angled in relation to each other, are the same.

LITERATURE

S.L. Huntington, *The "Pāla-Sena" Schools of Sculpture*, Leiden, 1984.

47
Votive *stūpa*, sandstone. Bodhgaya, 11th–12th century

Height $40\frac{1}{2}$ in. (103 cm.)
O.S. 59

Model *stupas* such as these are found in considerable numbers at Bodhgaya, the site of the Mahābodhi temple (see no.29), and at many other Buddhist monuments. They were placed there by monks or members of the laity, in the same way as the relief-steles depicting the Buddha, Bodhisattvas or other members of the Buddhist pantheon. In contrast to *ex votos* in Christian churches, which are usually presented in gratitude for answered prayers, the Buddhist equivalents were given as a means of acquiring merit not only for the donor but for his parents and, a phrase often recurring in inscriptions, all sentient beings.

These miniature *stūpas*, presumably small versions of the large ones, are precious documents in tracing the evolution of the latter, which have almost all disappeared. Instead of the low, barely hemispherical dome, on a low platform, of the earliest *stūpas* (see no.19), here the high stepped base, square in plan, supports a tall cylindrical section, only the topmost portion of which consists of a dome, its curved portion little more than a cap. The *harmikā*, the little platform fenced off by a *vedikā*, of the early *stūpas* has been stylised beyond all recognition; so has the parasol and its staff (*chattrāvalī*), now a thin truncated cone of seven compacted parasols. Small niches at the cardinal points on the base and larger ones on the cylindrical part of the *stūpa*, contain relief figures. Occasionally one of these is opened up, introducing a shrine element to the *stūpa*.

Figures of the Buddha are placed in three of the large niches (the fourth is empty). He is seated in *padmāsana* (see no.38) and the hands are in the *mudrās* (symbolic gestures) of meditation, preaching and "earth touching" (*bhūmisparśa*), the latter particularly appropriate since it recalls the Buddha, seated under the Bodhi tree at Bodhgaya, "calling the earth to witness" that he had overcome the demon Māra who had sought to prevent him from achieving Illumination. While these figures may therefore stand for three great events in the life of the historical Buddha (see nos.17 and 50), it is more likely, at this relatively late date when the doctrines of later Buddhism held sway in northern India, that they represent three of the Meditation Buddhas or Jinas (Dhyāni-Buddhas?) most appropriately placed, since these essentially metaphysical concepts came to incorporate directional symbolism.

Published photographs (see below) of almost identical miniature *stūpas* still *in situ* at Bodhgaya leave no doubt that the Museum's example comes from there, particularly since these are of a rather distinctive type. During cleaning and extensive "excavations" towards the end of the 19th century, hundreds and even thousands of these little monuments were taken away, many of them to Burma, the site having passed under the control of a Hindu religious organisation. The Museum possesses several other miniature *stūpas* from Bodhgaya.

LITERATURE

See M. Benisti, *Contribution à l'Etude du Stūpa Bouddhique Indien: Les Stūpa Mineurs de Bodh-gāya et de Ratnagiri*, Paris, 1981, pp.7–10 and figs.13–14.

48

Viṣṇu (the "Hedges" Viṣṇu), ceriticised slate (siltstone). Sagar Island, West Bengal; c.1050

Height 35 in. (89 cm.)
Pitt-Rivers Museum A.M. 169
Gift of Sir William Hedges, 1686–87

Steles of the latter part of the Pāla-Sena period (8th to 12th century), carved out of the characteristic dark siltstone from the Rajmahal hills in Bihar, are probably more numerously represented in museums than any other type of Indian sculptures, with the one exception of Gandhara work also in a highly characteristic stone. This representation of the god Viṣṇu is a particularly fine example, without a trace of damage. It is also an important document in the history of the dissemination of Indian art throughout the world.

The four-armed god stands, richly crowned and bejewelled in *samapada*, the rather rigid posture much favoured for central figures by Pāla sculptors. His upper right hands hold the mace and the discus, his lower left the conch and his lower right hand is outstretched in the boon-giving (*varada*) gesture with a lotus blossom carved on the palm. The long floral garland (*vanamālā*) usually adorning the god sweeps down to below his knees. Below the shoulders, the image of the god is actually cut out from the ground, a technique much favoured in this style.

Much of the interest of this sculpture derives from the rich carving of the surround, both because of the profusion of iconographic detail and the liveliness of the two attendant female figures, whose more sinuous poses compensate for the stiffness of the central figure. On the proper right is Śrī Devī, holding a fly-whisk, on the left Puṣṭi (Sarasvatī), holding a musical instru-

ment (here a *vīṇā*). At the top of the stele a small *kīrtimukha* (face of glory) gathers all the relief elements to a point. Below are two *vidyādharas*, holding shield and sword (see no.32); then, on each side, a vertical series of little panels depicting the various incarnations (*avatāras*) of Viṣṇu, at this period usually counted to be ten in number, including the Buddha and Kalki on his horse. Below Viṣṇu's double lotus pedestal is a minuscule Garuḍa and two equally minute figures, one of which is perhaps the donor.

Despite its condition and the particularly crisp quality of its carving, this Viṣṇu would only be regarded as one of many Pāla sculptures, imposing but somewhat metallic in their precision, were it not that its acquisition in 1686–7 by the newly founded Ashmolean Museum is documented in detail, along with its probable find-place. In 1690, *The Book of Benefactors* records in Latin that Sir William Hedges gave an image (*idolum*) of "Gonga" from a temple on the island of Saugor (or Sagar) at the mouth of the Ganges. The name "Gonga" was at first a stumbling block, since it suggests the goddess Gaṅgā, widely worshipped in Bengal, until passages in a mid-17th century treatise by a Dutch missionary indicated that amongst Europeans in eastern India, the name Ganga could refer to any Hindu male god or "devil". Moreover, Hedges, who for three turbulent years was governor of the East India Company in Bengal, kept a diary in which he records that on March 16, 1683, "We went in Budgeros [a kind of local boat] to see ye Pagodas at Sagor", which is indeed at the entrance to the Hooghly River, the mouth of the Ganges by which ships pass up to Calcutta. It is most likely that Hedges combined sightseeing on that day with a little collecting. Where in Bengal the image was carved is not known (the stone in any case had been transported from more than 200 miles away), although certain iconographic and stylistic traits indicate an origin in south-east Bengal or southern Bangladesh. What is certain is that Hedges had actually set foot on Saugor and that he was personally familiar with the kinds of images to be found there. An equally fine Pāla image (of Sūrya) in the Philadelphia Museum of Art is also believed to have come from Saugor.

So far as is known, this Pāla Viṣṇu is the first major Indian sculpture to have been acquired by a museum in the West and which can be identified today. Although it is on permanent public display in the Ashmolean Museum, it is officially on loan from another of Oxford University's museums, the Pitt-Rivers, having been transferred there during the rationalisation of 1886, long before the Department of Eastern Art was created in the Ashmolean.

PUBLISHED

J.C. Harle, "The 'Hedges' Viṣṇu", *Festschrift in Honour of Professor Dr. H. Härtel* (to appear).

49

Pair of stone pillars (pilasters), ceritised slate (siltstone). Probably from the Adina Mosque, Pandua, West Bengal, late 14th century

Height 43 in. (109.2 cm.)
X.2477 (a) and (b).

These two elaborately carved pillars are technically pilasters, since full-length portions of two adjacent sides remain uncarved. The Adina mosque at Pandua and the one at Gaur are the two earliest mosques to have survived in Bengal and unlike almost all their successors were built of stone. This was almost certainly thanks to the proximity of the Rajmahal hills in Bihar, the only source of stone for Bengal, both for building and for sculpture (see no.48). The decoration consists mostly of floral or abstract motifs, although bunches of grapes (?) as well as bells can be identified. These would be acceptable to Muslims; on the other hand, the general nature of the decoration belongs to the stylistic *koine* of late North Indian architectural decoration, Hindu ornament having become increasingly formalised to the point of abstraction. The earlier mosques in western India, dating from the 12th century, made extensive use of materials taken from demolished Hindu temples, which raises the intriguing possibility that these pillars were originally carved for a Hindu temple and re-used for the Adina Mosque.

There are identical pillars in the British Museum and the Royal Scottish Museum.

50
Buddhist votive plaque illustrating the eight great events of the Buddha's life, terracotta. Burma, probably Pagan, 13th century

Height $6\frac{1}{4}$ in. (15.9 cm.)
X.215

Buddhist terracotta votive plaques or tablets have been found in their thousands from Bodhgaya in Bihar to Pagan and other sites in Burma, as well as in Thailand and elsewhere. The practice of stamping out these depictions of the Buddha or scenes from the Buddha's life as a devotional practice, often so deep in the matrix as to form almost a miniature shrine, appears to have originated in Bodhgaya. Their iconography is dominated by the great Illumination and the style is that of Pāla Bihar and Bengal, so much so that it is often not possible to establish where a plaque, or rather the mould from which it was stamped, was actually made, particularly as the ubiquitous Buddhist creed, when stamped below the image, is written in the commonest classical Indian script, Devanāgarī. There is no question, moreover, that the seals travelled widely. Like votive *stūpas* (no.47), but portable, they could be used as a pious offering to a temple or carried home to a private shrine, a house or a monk's cell.

The Museum has a collection of over twenty votive plaques whose moulds can confidently be asserted to have been made in India, and usually at Bodhgaya, but the seal illustrated here, although showing strong Indian influence, is Burmese. The reason for this choice is primarily the unsurpassed crispness of detail and the beauty and interest of the little scenes depicted around the Buddha. Also, although the inscription is illegible, it can be assumed that it ended quite exceptionally, after the Buddhist creed, with the name of the person whose pious gift it was, in this case a man named Mahāsālini. Ordinarily, the donor is not named; on Burmese seals, dedicatory inscriptions, where they occur, are generally on the reverse, in one of the local languages.

Around the enshrined central figure of the Buddha achieving enlightenment are depicted (clockwise), though not in the order of their occurrence, the other seven great events of the Buddha's life: the monkey's offering of a bowl of honey, the first sermon, the taming of the mad elephant, the *Parinirvāṇa*, the descent from the heaven of the thirty-three gods, the miracle of Śrāvasti and the birth. The little upturned eaves of the Buddha's towered shrine are unmistakably Burmese.

LITERATURE

Examples of the "Mahāsālini" plaque: G.H. Luce, *Old Burma – Early Pagan*, 3 vols., New York, 1969–70, pls.71, a, b, c. 74, a, c; W. Zwalf, ed. *Buddhism, Art and Faith*, British Museum exhibition catalogue, 1985, no.223; S.D. Lawson, "A Catalogue of Indian Buddhist Clay Sealings in British Museums", unpublished D.Phil. thesis, Oxford, 1982.

51

Yoga-Narasiṃha, the man-lion incarnation of Viṣṇu, Narasiṃha, in the yogāsana position, stone. Orissa, 14th–16th century

Height $16\frac{1}{8}$ in. (50 cm.)
1966.88

Orissa was one of the regions of northern India that continued longest to produce sculpture in stone and bronze (see no.52) which was both original in conception and of a high degree of technical competence. The adjacent region of Bengal had introduced during the later Pāla period the technique of cutting away all the stone ground around the body and head of an image. Here the process has been carried to the extreme so that what remains of the ground more nearly resembles the halo (*prabhāmaṇḍala*) surrounding a metal image, except for the flat top with the head of the god projecting beyond it. The head is a fine example of inventive caricature, hardly leonine at all, with its hook nose and upturned moustaches. A very similar lion-head can be seen on the superb ivory throne leg from Orissa, now in the Seattle Museum of Art, similarly monstrous, but with the same mad geniality, the Indian sculptor invariably treating even his most grotesque creations with sympathy. The man-lion's mane is shown, in a delightfully fanciful way, cascading down in a series of ringlets on either side of his crown.

The god sits cross-legged in the *yogāsana* position (sometimes called *utkuṭaka*), with a band to hold both knees. His lower hands are stretched forward and rest on his knees, his upper ones hold the discus and the conch as befits an incarnation of Viṣṇu. This "single" (*kevala*) image of Narasiṃha is comparatively rare. Far more common are those showing the man-lion disembowelling Hiraṇyakaśipu, one of the most terrible of the *Daityas*.

52 COLOUR PLATE 8

Seated Gaṇeśa, gilded bronze. Orissa, 16th century

Height $4\frac{1}{4}$ in. (10.8 cm.)
1980.64
Gift of Douglas and Mary Barrett

Like the previous figure, this bronze attests to the continuing high quality of work produced in Orissa at a relatively late date. There are indeed striking similarities with the stone image, as in the imaginative treatment of the hair (a wig?) which sits on top of Gaṇeśa's head. Unquestionably made of hair, it resembles at the same time the multi-layered roofs of many of the temple buildings in Orissa.

Gaṇeśa, according to the *Purāṇas*, is the son of Śiva and Pārvatī, although his relationship with his mother is particularly close. One of the most popular of all Indian deities, he is the god of wisdom and learning, the bestower of wealth and above all the remover of obstacles (Vighneśvara). As such he is worshipped before any new undertaking, and at the beginning of all religious observances except funeral rites.

Accounts differ as to how he got his elephant head and why one of his tusks is always shown broken off.

The elephant-headed god sits in a rare position (see no.1) on a lotus-petalled throne, with his vehicle, a mouse (or shrew) on the base looking up at him. In his right upper hand he holds the elephant goad (*aṅkuśa*), in the left a hooded serpent. His sacred thread (*yajño-pavīta*) is likewise a serpent which indicates his connection with Śiva. His lower left hand holds a bowl full to the brim with little round cakes, of which Gaṇeśa is believed to be inordinately fond. The end of his trunk, which is turned to the left, is about to pick up one of the cakes. His lower right hand holds what is almost certainly the end of his broken tusk. The Ashmolean's bronze is closely related to the magnificent ivory Gaṇeśa from Orissa, now in the Metropolitan Museum, New York, although smaller and probably a century or so later in date. The bases are similar, as is the shape of the ears, and the elaborate and distinctive dressing of the hair, referred to above, is almost identical in both sculptures. The dressing of the hair furthermore continues in the same highly distinctive fashion at the back of the head, where three widely separated tresses diverge and hang down to the waist. From the waist band also, on either side of both images, hang heavy tassels of a particularly Orissan shape.

LITERATURE

A. de Lippe, *The Freer Indian Sculptures*, Washington, D.C., 1970, figs.53–55.

53

Head, probably of a Jain Tīrthaṅkara, reddish buff sandstone. Probably north-west Madhya-Pradesh, region of Jhansi; 11th–12th century

Height 11 in. (28 cm.)
X.245

This detached head, with its exquisitely sensitive modelling, shows to what extent, even in the later Hindu period, tactile values of the highest order can be accommodated within a highly stylised conception. The median parting of the snail curls provides a strong vertical axis, from which the curls, in unusual wave-like patterns, appear to rush away. Perfectly ordered, their rows upon rows suggest nonetheless a rough turbulence which offsets any hint of effeteness in the smooth surfaces of the face below, over which the thin line of the eyebrows appears to wander with a life of its own. The emotional impact of this head, which is powerful, then emanates from the barely adumbrated depressions, even dimples, around the mouth and the lower part of the nose.

The head was almost certainly part of a stele and most likely had a halo. The pupils of the eyes are indicated by incised lines.

LITERATURE

S. Kramrisch, *The Hindu Temple*, 2 vols. Calcutta, 1946, pl.LVIII.

54
Vāsudeva(?), Subhadrā and Balarāma (fragment), red sandstone. Rajasthan or Madhya Pradesh, 11th–12th century

Height $19\frac{1}{4}$ in. (48.9 cm.)
1961.68

This little group, including the small donor figure, stood at the base, on one side, of the surround of a large image, most likely Viṣṇu. Such elaborately carved surrounds are a feature of large stele after the Gupta period and with their superimposed figures and motifs and elaborate symbolism they have much in common with the doorways of the period (see no.55).

The figures are easily recognizable as Kṛṣṇa, holding the discus in his right hand, or more likely Vāsudeva, because of his crown, Subhadrā, holding what appears to be a lotus, and Balarāma, identifiable by the *hala* (plough) he is holding and his serpent hood. They are thus clearly representative, even at this comparatively late date, of members of the family group of five folk heroes at the origin of much of the cult of Viṣṇu (see no.14). Their relation to the iconographical grouping known as Ekānaṃśa ("the single portionless, or undivided one"), with the goddess as the central figure, cannot be discerned in this fragmentary context.

55
Portion of a door-jamb, light buff sandstone. Rajasthan or Madhya Pradesh, 11th–12th century

Height 31 in. (78.7 cm.)
O.S. 71

The doors through which Indian temples are entered, and particularly the entrance to the *garbha-gṛha* containing the *liṅga* or the principal image of the shrine, have a specially important place in the multiple symbolism of the temple. Through them the worshipper, either in person or through the surrogate form of a priest, makes a final entrance into the realm of the unmanifest or the divine. In consequence, jambs, lintel, even the doorstep, are richly carved with reliefs of divinities, guardians and auspicious figures, each in their proper place and enclosed by multiple bands of parallel mouldings, sometimes of the greatest beauty, which frame the doorway.

Here, in the rather simplified style characteristic of this late period, a male and female pair (*mithuna*) stand at the base in an emphasised flexed position. Since the man holds an emblem (difficult to identify), and the woman a lotus, they may in fact be gods. Above, musicians playing drums or cymbals are placed in small panels, each topped by a little triangular motif, the ultimate stylisation of the *caitya* arch or *gavākṣa* (see no.13). The moulding running up beside the panels again represents the final reduction to the simplest terms of the splendid fan-palm mouldings of the Gupta period. The small figure with his hands pressed together in *añjali*, the gesture of worshipful respect, is a common feature. His snake-body, here not completed, would normally run up and across the lintel to meet its counterpart from the other doorway jamb, the tails often being held in the beak of Garuḍa, Viṣṇu's bird vehicle.

56

Umā-maheśvara or Hara-gaurī, brass. Rajasthan, probably Jalor, 1283

Height $9\frac{1}{8}$ in. (23.2 cm.)
1965.5

This brass image is closely related in iconography to the small stone stele illustrated as no.45; its quality, however, is considerably greater. Umā is a proud little figure and the Nandī has real individuality. The exceptionally thin legs and the slim body of both the central figures add a touch of elegance to this sculpture. They are, moreover, admirably set off by the spare but beautifully proportioned architectural surround.

The god holds a sweet lime (*mātuluṅga*), one of his emblems, in his lower right hand; the attendant figures are less numerous than in no.45, Bhṛṅgi and Umā's lion being absent. A charming touch is the *épergne* heaped with sweet cakes, his favourite food, which is placed near Gaṇeśa. Another such object, on the centre of the base, is missing.

While Jain brasses from Rajasthan or Gujarat of the later Hindu period almost all bear long inscriptions detailing who they were made by and where, as well as a date (see no.57), inscribed Hindu images such as this one are rare at this time. Plastically, this image has escaped the trend towards excessive abstraction in geometric forms of the Jain images as seen in no. 57.

Mr. M.A. Dhaky of the American Institute of Indian Studies at Rām Nagar, Varanasi, has kindly supplied a transliteration and English translation of the image's inscription:

> Saṃvat 1340 varṣe Caitra vadi 13 Guravadyeha . . . śrīmad . . . jāla śrīnnatasavapādānāma (?) . . . mahārājye śrī Jābālapure samtiṣṭhamāna deva śrī Cāpaleśvara melakamahotsava . . . bhrati // nandatā . . . pūjyamāna . . . // "In the saṃvat (year) 1340, in Caitra, the thirteenth of the dark half and on Thursday, in the great kingdom of . . . at the festival of the god Cāpaleśvara at Śrī Jābālapura . . . (rest too fragmentary)."

Jābālapura is the ancient town of Jālor, in Rajasthan, near Mt. Abu.

METAL ANALYSIS
Iron: trace; Copper 69.1; Zinc: 26.7; Lead: 1.3; Tin: 1.4; Antimony 0.23.

PUBLISHED
In the Image of Man ed. G. Michell, Exhib. Cat., London, 1982, no.441 (not illustrated).

57

Seated Image of the Jain Tīrthaṅkara Kunthunātha, brass with copper and silver inlay. "Vasantapuranagara", made in 1476

Height $7\frac{15}{16}$ in. (20.2 cm.)
O.S. 108
Presented by Mrs. Luard in 1936

Just as the historical Gautama Buddha came to be seen by later adherents of the faith he founded as only one of a long line of former Buddhas, so the historical Mahāvīra, founder of the Jaina faith, came to be counted as the twenty-fourth Tīrthaṅkara (literally "ford-maker") or great teacher of that religion. The present image is a representation of Śrī Kunthunātha, the seventeenth in the line.

A comprehensive inscription on the back of the image states that it was commissioned by a certain merchant Simghāka together with his wife and two brothers, and was installed by Śāstrī Lakṣmīsāgarasūri, a monk of the sixth *gaccha* (tapāgaccha) of the Śvetāṃbara or white-clad branch of the Jain faith. It was made in the town of Vasantapura, one of the major centres of Jainism at this time as attested in works such as Hemacandra's *Pariśiṣṭaparvan*, which corresponds to the modern Vasantagaḍh in southern Rajasthan, where other bronze Jaina images dating from as early as the 7th century A.D. have been found.

Amongst the small attendant figures in the *prabhāvali* are doubtless the *yakṣa* and *yakṣī* associated with Kunthunātha, the latter the only recognisable female figure, seated in *lalitāsana*. There is the outline of a goat, Kunthunātha's *vāhana*, lightly etched on a panel below the seated figure. Otherwise the little figures have no distinguishing marks or attributes, and are stylised to an extraordinary degree into the quasi-geometrical forms of the late Western Indian Jain style.

The Ashmolean possesses another almost identical image (O.S.110), also of Kunthunātha, consecrated in 1470 by the same Lakṣmīsāgara.

PUBLISHED

Maj. C.E. Luard, "A Collection of Brass from Central India", *Journal of Indian Art and Industry, XVI, 1914*, pl.10 and pp.115–16 with a full translation of the inscription. For a brief notice of Lakṣmīsāgarasūri see, *Indian Antiquary XI*, 256, no.53 (Sept. 1882).

58

Lakṣmī-Nārāyaṇa, greenish-black serpentine, traces of plaster. Western India, probably Southern Rajasthan, dated 1495

Height $17\frac{3}{4}$ in. (45 cm.)
1965.161

Nārāyaṇa is one of the many forms of Viṣṇu, and Lakṣmī, goddess of wealth, is his consort. Although in a late provincial style, not without folk elements (for example the treatment of the faces and the god's hand), this image is in a sense a Vaiṣṇava companion piece to the stone and brass Umā-Maheśvara images (nos.45, 56), an illustration of the parallelism which can so often be noted between the iconographies of the two great theistic cults. In each image the god is seated in *lalitāsana* (see nos.45 and 56), with his consort seated on his knee and clasped by his left arm. In each, the vehicle (here Garuḍa, the man-bird) is placed below. The iconography of the metal image is more elaborate; attendant figures here are limited to the donor, the small figure with his hands in *añjali*.

Viṣṇu wears the cylindrical crown particular to him. He holds the club in his upper right hand and the *cakra* (wheel or discus) in his left. His lower right hand, extended downwards in a gesture simulating *varada* ("bestowing a boon or gift"), holds an *akṣamālā* (rosary made of seeds) stretched out over the fingers.

Mr. M.A. Dhaky of the American Institute of Indian Studies at Rām Nagar, Varanasi, has kindly supplied a transliteration and English translation of the image's inscription:

> Svasti śrī saṃvat 1552 va(rṣe) Āṣāḍhamāse śakula(=śukla)pakṣe caturdasyām 14 // . . . -ṣāḍhānakṣatre . . . //
>
> In the saṃvat year 1552 on the 14th of the bright half of the month of Āṣādha . . . in the constellation of (Pūrvā-/Uttarā-)ṣāḍhā . . . (rest too fragmentary).

LITERATURE

J.E. Van Lohuizen-de Leeuw, *Indian Sculptures in the Van der Heydt Collection*, Zurich, 1964, nos.33–4.

59

Kṛṣṇa Govardhanadharaṇa (Kṛṣṇa holding up the Govardhana mountain), black marble. Rajasthan, 15th–16th century

Height 18 in. (45.7 cm.)
1980.2
Purchased with the help of the Victoria and Albert Museum Purchase Grant Fund; formerly Goulandris collection.

Kṛṣṇa, the cow-herd god, and a form of Viṣṇu/Vāsudeva (see nos.14 and 54) was originally a folk-hero famous for his exploits both as a child and a young man. These are extensively portrayed in friezes, in miniature painting and, in South India, in bronze (see no.69). Only one of these themes, however, figures in large sculptural panels or free-standing sculpture; it portrays Kṛṣṇa holding up the mountain Govardhana ("increaser of kine") near Mathura so that the cowherds and their flocks can shelter from a seven-day storm sent by Indra, anciently the warrior chief of the gods, whose worship was being neglected by Kṛṣṇa and his companions.

This unusual sculpture is from Rajasthan, a region particularly devoted to the cult of Kṛṣṇa and where a late flowering in sculpture and architecture took place, particularly in Mewar (Udaipur) in the 15th and 16th centuries.

The peculiar shape of the mountain is no doubt an echo of the simile used in the *Bhāgavata-Purāṇa*, the principal source of the Kṛṣṇa legend, when "Kṛṣṇa plucked the Govardhana mountain with one hand and held it up playfully as a child might a mushroom". Instead of the rustication usually employed by Indian sculptors to depict a mountain or mountainous terrain, the "stem" is decorated in a plant-like manner. The base and the "head" of the mushroom-mountain are etched with outline figures of devotees, cattle, birds including peacocks, and vegetation. Little more than graffiti, these may have been added later.

LITERATURE

See *Bhāgavata-Purāṇa*, trans. N. Raghunathan, 2 vols., Madras, 1976, Book 10, ch.25., *ibid*, II, p.25.

60

Yoginīmukha, grey sandstone (lower part of neck made up). Rajasthan or Gujarat, 17th–18th century

Height 16 in. (40.6 cm.)
1965.41

In Indian art, most detached heads sculptured in stone have been broken off their bodies, as in the case of nos.12, 30, 38, 53. In Rajasthan or Gujarat, however,

heads such as this one replaced the tip of the central spine of each of the four sides of the *śikhara* ("tower") of the "northern" type shrines built at a relatively late date. They are called *yoginīmukhas* (*yoginī* heads) and presumably represent one of the minor female deities or demonesses who follow Durga. In certain other parts of India, lions or other figures occupy this position.

The style or approximations to it is most often seen in small brass heads from the same regions of western India and, except for folk art (there are traces of folk style here), represents the final purely Indian stylistic development there before the admixture of European elements.

61

Kurmāvatara (the tortoise incarnation of Viṣṇu), bronze, solid cast. Bombay or Gujarat, dated 1801

Height $15\frac{3}{8}$ in. (39 cm.)
1967.43
Formerly collection J.R. Belmont, Basel

Viṣṇu's second avatāra, when he served as the pivot or support for the churning stick when the gods and the *asuras*, using the serpent Vāsuki as a rope, churned the ocean of milk. This is one of the principal Indian creation myths. Viṣṇu is usually represented, as here, with a human upper body. He holds his usual attributes, the *cakra*, or discus (here bent back), the conch-shell, the club and the lotus.

There is a short two line inscription in Sanskrit on the base, which reads:

> // Śrī Kūrmasevakaś Cedipatiḥ Kūrmapālaḥ //
> Jaiṣṭaśukla // 8 // Saṃ // 1858 (?) // muḥkāsī // *(sic.)*

The final word of the inscription is obscure.

62

Durgā Mahiṣāsuramardinī, bronze. Deccan, c.900 A.D.

Height $3\frac{11}{16}$ in. (9.4 cm.)
1980.62

In spite of its small size, this is a notable bronze in its own right, while showing a further development in the iconography of images depicting Durgā slaying the *asura* Mahiṣa, the demon buffalo (see no. 31). The body of the buffalo, although brought to its knees, is horizontal, and its head has been cut off. Through the gaping hole in the neck there emerges the *asura* (demon) in human form, to be despatched by Durgā's trident. *Asuras* were capable of assuming various forms, human as well as animal, and there is textual authority for the final emergence of the demon as a man from the slain buffalo.

The goddess has sixteen arms. Already in the 5th century, a famous rock-cut image shows her with ten, and the number of arms of some Indian images tends to increase with the centuries. They are particularly necessary in the case of Durgā slaying Mahiṣa, so as to accommodate the panoply of weapons and symbols provided by the gods for her combat. Prominent among them are Viṣṇu's most customary emblems, the conch shell and the discus, here shown as a ring. The lion, near the buffalo's hindquarters, has joined in the fray while Durgā, as so often in images of the Goddess in *ugra* (angry) form, wears a beatific smile.

63

Vīrabhadra, brass with inlays. Karnataka, 16th–17th century

Height $6\frac{3}{4}$ in. (17 cm.)
1964.157
Given by Mr. H.L. Dunkley

Vīrabhadra is an emanation of Śiva, created to wreak havoc on Dakṣa's sacrifice. Dakṣa was the father of Śiva's first wife, Satī, who objected to their union because of Śiva's constant attendance at cemeteries and burning grounds, as well as his appearance, smeared with ashes and with unkempt hair, and his wild behaviour. Unable to prevent Śiva's marriage to Satī (Pārvatī, in another version), Dakṣa planned a great sacrifice to which he pointedly did not invite Śiva. When Satī's pleadings that he should not dishonour her in this way were ignored, she leapt into the sacrificial fire and was consumed by the flames (hence the name given to the rite where Hindu widows threw themselves on to their husband's funeral pyre). Śiva, distraught with grief and fury, wreaked terrible destruction on the sacrifice and in the process cut off Dakṣa's head. Eventually Śiva repented and brought Dakṣa back to life, but his head could not be found, and a goat's head was substituted for it. Hindu myths indeed rarely have an unhappy final outcome; disastrous occurrences are as often as not remedied by one or other of the gods although, perhaps influenced by the Indian cyclical view of time, a further episode is always possible.

Images of Vīrabhadra and temples dedicated to him are particularly common in Andhra and Karnataka. Here he stands in a curious pose, his weight evenly distributed on both legs, slightly bent at the knees and with the feet wide apart. He holds a trident in his rear left hand and a shield (*kheṭaka*) resting on a human

head (presumably that of Dakṣa) in his lower right. This is in accordance with the prescriptive texts. His lower right hand is clenched so as to hold a removable object (here missing), most likely a bow or arrow or a sword (*khaḍga*). In his upper left hand he holds what may be a *ḍamaru* (a word of Tamil origin for a small hour-glass shaped drum, common in the iconography of the Tamil region, but apparently not mentioned in the texts as an attribute of Vīrabhadra). The sandals, with a projecting knob gripped between the big and first toe, are associated in Tamilnadu with Śiva as ascetic and mendicant.

Vīrabhadra is an *ugra* (wrathful) aspect of the god, as indicated by the long wreath of skulls (*muṇḍamālā*) reaching down below his knees and the head hanging down on a long cord from his waist. This could conceivably represent a strand of hair, Vīrabhadra having been created, according to one version of the myth, from one of Śiva's matted locks. The curved sword, here stuck into Vīrabhadra's belt, is also one of his common symbols. He wears a tall *mukuṭa* (much rubbed, like his face). His eyes are inlaid with silver and there are individual inlays of very small rubies, many of them missing.

On Vīrabhadra's right stands Dakṣa, with a goat or sheep's head and his hands held in *añjali*. On his (proper) left sits the small but carefully modelled female figure of Bhadrakālī, by one account the leader of Vīrabhadra's armies. She sits atop two (three?) superimposed inverted triangles whose significance is not clear. Two little couchant Nandīs (see no.64) occupy the outer corners of the base, which is of some complexity.

There is a fine *prabhāmaṇḍala* (aureole) with the typical vegetal scrolls winding up on either side, the three top circles enclosing a lion, a *kīrtimukha* (lion mask, lit.: "face of glory") and a *yāḷi*, a mythical animal commonly depicted in later Indian art, sometimes called a leogryph in English. The outermost band of the aureole, a sort of bead and reel, springs from the mouths of two small animal figures, their front paws propped on the top ledge of the base. The back of the aureole is also decorated with incised patterns.

Metal sculpture from the Deccan is relatively rare and this image has the added interest of being inscribed in Canarese characters of the 16th–17th centuries. The inscription reads: *Devabhāṇu mādi dānu*: "Devabhāṇu made me". The name Vīrabhadra simply means "distinguished hero".

64 COLOUR PLATE 9

Nandī, granite. Deccan or South India, 16th–17th century

Height 22 in. (55.9 cm.) Length 27½ in. (69.9 cm.)
Width 16 in. (40.6 cm.)
O.S. 77

The humped bull (*bos indicus*) has always been a favourite with Indian artists, going back to the engravers of the Indus Valley seals. After the Gupta period, Nandī, the bull, becomes intimately associated with Śiva as his "vehicle". This is the rather unfortunate translation of the Sanskrit word *vāhana* denoting the animal or bird which is particular to a divinity and on which he or she sits or rides. Viṣṇu's *vāhana* is Gāruḍa, an anthropomorphised bird (see no.58), and that of Brahmā, the goose (haṃsa) (see no.40).

It is, however, as a large sculpture in the round of a young couchant bull, usually placed facing a Śiva temple, that Nandī is best known. Nearly every one of the thousands of temples has its Nandī and there is a gigantic example outside the city of Mysore. He is invariably portrayed, whatever the size of the sculpture, as a young bull, his horns mere stumps, caparisoned with bands, chains or garlands and hung with bells. His pose varies little and, however conventionalised the style of the carving, there rarely fails to emanate from it the deep sympathy, based on close

observations, which the Indian sculptor of every age never fails to show for animals. Here, the tongue licking the nostril is a small but compelling touch.

PUBLISHED

In the Image of Man, ed. G. Michell, Exhib. Cat., London 1982, p.215.

65

Viṣṇu, grey granite. Late Pallava, Tamilnadu, South India, 9th–10th century

Height 36 in. (91.5 cm.)
1981.10
Purchased with the help of a grant from the E.H. North Bequest

This fine stele represents the god Viṣṇu, easily identifiable by his tall cylindrical crown (*kirīṭa-mukuṭa*) and the discus and conch held in his rear hands. The large size of these emblems and the small flames sprouting from them, as well as the discus turned endwise, are all stylistic marks of the end of the Pallava period (7th–9th centuries), as is the little strip of material sticking up from the topmost belt. The outline of the stele follows that of the figure.

The god stands stiff-legged and wears an ankle-length, transversely pleated *dhoti*, the man's lower garment still worn by vast numbers of Indians today. There are three belts, the upper apparently jewelled and the lower (presumably of cloth) having outward-flowing side-ribbons and an ankle-length pleated strip hanging down on each side. The god wears a sacred thread (*yajñopavīta*) and stomach band (*udarabandha*); the former has a clasp by the shoulder and one strand joins the stomach band. Jewellery includes triangular foliate ear-rings, armlets (*keyūras*) with a central circular portion from which rise three jewelled spikes, a single broad necklace and three plain bracelets on each wrist.

Monuments and sculpture in stone only appear in Tamilnadu in the 7th century, although their degree of stylistic development implies a previous tradition in perishable materials. Images of this type, both cut out of the living rock or in high relief on stele, thus stand fairly close to the emergence of the style which was to be continued so brilliantly under the early Coḷas. Due to its late appearance and the intense conservatism of sculptural style in South India (indeed through the whole Coḷa period that ends c.1250 A.D., there are no radical departures), the history of style in Tamilnadu follows a very different rhythm from that in other parts of India.

66

Gaurī, bronze (solid cast). Tamilnadu, c.14th century

Height 22 in. (55.9 cm.), including base
1958.205A
Oswald J. Couldrey Bequest

The famous bronzes of Tamilnadu are as a rule solid cast, unlike other Indian bronzes, which are hollow cast. The figure is modelled in clay and simply covered with a coating of wax, whereas in solid casting the figure itself is modelled in wax. In both cases, the wax is replaced by the metal, the process known as *cire-perdue* casting, for which the Sanskrit term *madhūcchiṣṭa* (wasted honey) is an exact equivalent. It is still practised today.

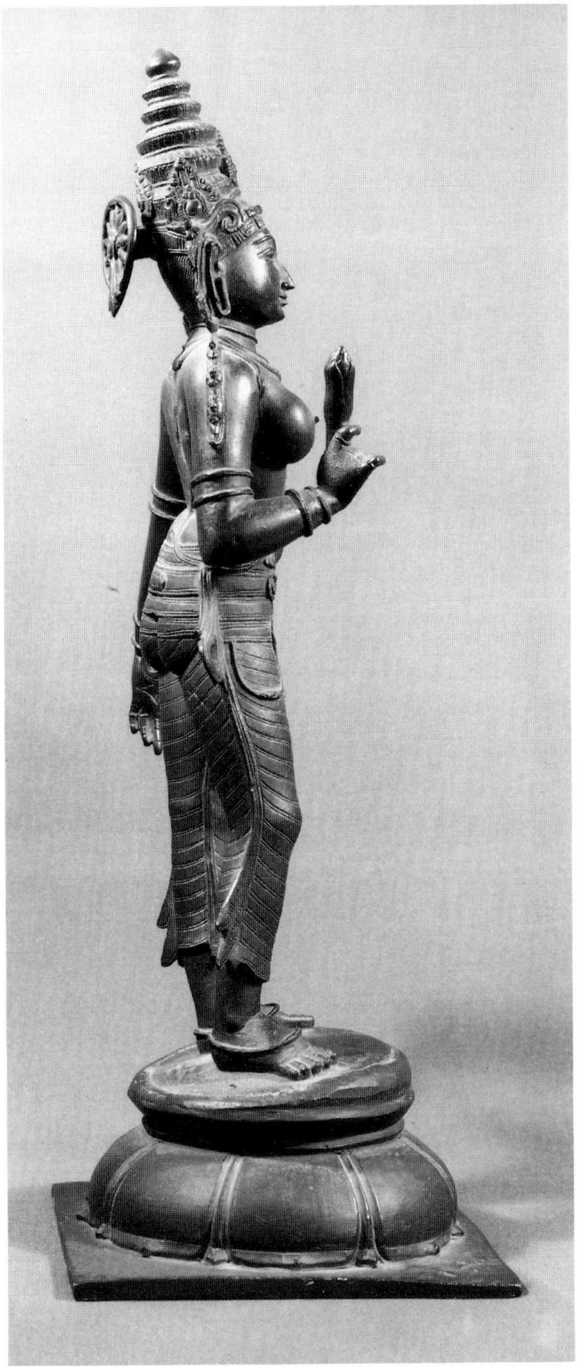

Tamilnadu bronzes are distinguished by their simplicity of composition, usually comprising a single figure, sometimes two, a god and his consort, and, rarely, three; Śiva's bull is also sometimes included, not in miniature but on the same scale as the other figures. There are generally no aureoles or subsidiary figures. Individual figures range from not much more than inch-high to up to three feet. In fact more sizable images in bronze were produced in Tamilnadu than in any other part of India.

The great age of bronze sculpture in Tamilnadu was from the 9th to the middle of the 11th century, when the later Pallavas and early Coḷas ruled. Many of these works are unsurpassed anywhere in the world for their gracefulness, perfect proportions, and quiet assurance. In no other culture have the gods been portrayed so appealingly in human form.

Gaurī is a particularly gentle and benevolent form of Pārvatī. Her right hand holds a lotus in bud, her left hangs at the end of a drooping and slightly out-thrust arm in the *mudrā* known as *lolahastamudrā*. The portrayal of feminine costume and adornment, although slightly simplified, has barely changed since the 10th century and the proud set of the youthful head, in side view, which is reminiscent of the finest Coḷa sculpture, makes it difficult to date this sculpture accurately. The exaggerated *bhaṅga* (*déhanchement*) of the body, the way it is conceived in sections, seen full face, and a general hardness of plastic treatment, as well as the summary execution of some of the features of the face, unmistakably point to a late date.

67

Tirumaṅkai Āḻvār, bronze (solid cast). Tamilnadu, 15th century

Height $22\frac{5}{8}$ in. (57.5 cm.)
1967.42
Formerly J.R. Belmont Collection

The icons of Indian art usually represent gods, demigods or creatures of myth. Nonetheless, although to a lesser degree than in the West, images have also been made since at least the 6th century of holy men, great teachers and especially ardent devotees, particularly in South India. The Museum's collection includes a seated bronze figure of a Vaiṣṇava teacher (*ācārya*) perhaps Rāmānuja, the great theologian and philosopher (no. X.2387). Most commonly represented of all, however, are the Śaiva Nāyanārs (see no.68) and the Vaiṣṇava saints called Āḻvārs (7th–10th centuries). Tirumaṅkai Āḻvār, depicted here, is one of the most famous of these Tamil saints and hymnists; reformed bandit or highwayman, he is always depicted holding a sword and a shield. The sectarian mark known as the *ūrdhva-puṇḍra* engraved on his forehead and the little discus (*cakra*) and conch-shell on his shoulders leave no doubt as to the Vaiṣṇava affiliation of this image.

Although the legs are rather summarily treated – the shinbones coming to a point in front, in what has been likened to a fish's roe, facilitating this the image is not without dignity; and the rear, as so often in South Indian images, is tautly modelled. Small holes in the base are for the insertion of iron rods so that the image can be carried in procession.

68

Two piers from a miniature model of Tirumala Nāyak's *maṇḍapa* (hall), bronze (solid cast). Madura, Tamilnadu, 17th–18th century

Height $9\frac{9}{16}$ in. (24.3 cm.)
1956.673 & 674
Rev. W. Bentinck Hawkins Bequest, 1894

Models of sacred buildings have a long history in Indian art, commencing with reliquaries in the form of little *stūpas* (no.19). A number of small stone replicas of the Mahābodhi temple are known and the Museum has a small model bronze shrine, probably from southern Karnataka, on loan. These bronze piers, accurate in every detail, beautifully cast and exquisitely chased, belonged to a small-scale replica of one of the great pillared halls (*maṇḍapas*) which increasingly, from the Vijayanagara period (14th–16th centuries) onwards, became one of the principal features of the great temples of Tamilnadu. Other piers, probably parts of the same replica, are in the Victoria and Albert Museum, complete with corbels and linking architrave. In the same museum, detailed drawings made c.1801–5 to exactly the same

scale as the bronzes leave no doubt that the piers are from a replica of the *Pudu-maṇḍapa* of the Sundarésvara, the great temple of Madura in the far south of India. Indeed, the exact position of the two piers in the *maṇḍapa* of which the bronzes are models, amongst the total of more than one hundred and twenty, can be ascertained from the drawings.

Popularly called Tirumala Nāyak's "choultry" (shed or hall used by pilgrims, or for the transaction of public business), the Pudu or Vasanta (spring) *maṇḍapa* has long been one of the most famous buildings in India. Its builder (1623–1659) was the outstanding monarch, famous for his building activities, of the Nāyak dynasty of Madura, which ruled from the mid-16th to mid-18th centuries and has given its name to the most distinctive style of the final phase of traditional sculpture and architecture in Tamilnadu. For what purpose this model of Tirumala Nāyak's famous *maṇḍapa* was made is not clear. So far, it has not been possible to link the previous owner of the Ashmolean's two piers with Lord William Cavendish Bentinck (1774–1839), Governor of Madras (1803) and Governor-General of India (1833).

Each pier has a rich and carefully coordinated iconography linking the large end figures to the many smaller relief figures below and on the sides. For example, at one end of the pier on the left (1956.674) stands a four-armed Śiva. His two rear hands hold the axe and the deer, almost obligatory for South Indian Śivas, his right hand is in the gesture of teaching (*vyākhyāna-mudrā*), but in his left hand nestles, quite exceptionally, a bird. This presumably refers to a local Madura myth according to which Śiva taught a magic spell (*mantra*) to a blackbird for protection against stronger species. Hence birds peck at the flowered wreath suspended from the top of Śiva's crown and on one side of the pier the decoration consists largely of birds and foliage, while below stand little figures of the Nāyaṉārs (Śaiva saints), whose devotional hymns are still sung or recited daily for instructional purposes in the great Śiva temples of the south.

On the other hand, the pier on the right (1956.673) has an *ugra* (angry or baleful) eight-armed image of Kālī, with fangs, and the smaller figures below and on the side of the pier are also related to her, female dancers and musicians with hair erect on their heads and even fearsome figures waving a shield and sword, and one with pendulous breasts.

The style of these miniatures, modelled with such meticulous accuracy and attention to detail, unerringly reproduces the style of the originals, that of the Nāyak period based on the far south, with its occasional retention of some of the folk elements absorbed by the preceding Vijayanagara style; but in the main it is notable for its precision and naturalism, echoing in many ways the sculpture of the Coḷa period, but with a new hardness. Faces are often thin, with markedly aquiline features. The elaborately pleated skirt worn by Kālī is a feature of feminine costume in Nāyak times.

LITERATURE

J. Fergusson, *History of Indian and Eastern Architecture*, London, 1910, pp.386–90, figs.226–9; T.A. Gopinatha Rao, *Elements of Hindu Iconography*, Madras, 1916, V.2, pt.2, p.409.

69

Vaṭapatraśāyī Kṛṣṇa (Kṛṣṇa lying on the banyan leaf), bronze (solid cast). Tamilnadu, 17th–18th century

Length $10\frac{1}{4}$ in. (26 cm.)
1958.175
Oswald J. Couldrey Bequest

Kṛṣṇa as a baby, lying on his back on a banyan leaf (missing here) and sucking his toe, is a popular image in South India. Many of the cowherd god's exploits related in the *Bhāgavata-Purāṇa* (see no.59) were performed while he was still an infant. In fact, while still in the womb he was able to overcome his adversaries. The Museum possesses several small bronzes of Kṛṣṇa while still at the crawling stage. He is shown having just stolen the butter, one of his childish pranks. Here, however, he is younger still but nonetheless stands for the Supreme Viṣṇu, an interesting example of a tendency amongst all Indian religions, in their later phases, to share the same types of metaphysical speculation, in this case the identification of the supreme principle (compare the Ādi-Buddha of Mahāyāna Buddhism) underlying all the cosmological and philosophical manifestations of the god with an iconographically defined image, in this case, and quite appropriately, a naked infant.

While in northern and particularly western India, the treatment of the human body in sculpture in the later periods tends to an acute angularity and exaggerated poses, in South India, outlines of drawings favour flowing arcs and circles (see no.77) and in sculpture the use of globular masses is often the rule. The latter, as one sees here, are eminently suited to the plastic forms of a chubby baby.

FOLK BRONZES, PAINTINGS AND RITUAL OBJECTS

70

Liṅga shrine with Śiva and Pārvatī, brass. Madhya Pradesh (Central India), 17th–19th century

Height 3 in. (7.6 cm.)
X.2290

In Indian art, music and literature the Great Tradition or classical mainstream (*mārg*) espoused by noble, wealthy or urban patrons was accompanied by a vigorous Little Tradition of folk or vernacular (*deśī*) production, and a fertile interaction constantly occurred between the two. In the visual arts, surviving examples of folk sculptures and paintings are normally of a late date, though they clearly embody traditions that are centuries and even millennia old. This small household image was possibly made in Central India for tribals of the aboriginal Gond people, among whom Śiva (Mahādeo) is worshipped along with numerous local gods and spirits, being invoked especially by those wishing to have children. The divine couple Śiva and Pārvatī are rendered not with the graceful, sinuous volumes of classical sculpture, but with a powerful simplicity, recalling the primitive forms of autochthonous tribal deities.

The almost identical, goggle-eyed figures of Śiva and Pārvatī stand, with Śiva's trident between them, at one side of an altar platform rimmed by a twisted cable and set on a conical stand, with a *liṅga* and *yoni* at its centre. The main features of the shrine are defined by the spiralling forms of twisted and coiled wire, including the large, awesome faces and tall crowns of the two gods, whose trunks are simple posts carrying these convolutions. "The sanctuary is compacted of the memories of several techniques of an incipient metal age, of twisting grass and reeds, of shaping balls of clay. While the small *liṅga* is the centre of the sanctuary, the gods loom large in this concretion and adaptation of tribal memories to the worship of the *liṅga* and Śiva and Pārvatī" (Kramrisch).

PUBLISHED

S. Kramrisch, *Manifestations of Shiva*, Exhib. Cat., Philadelphia, 1981, no.102; compare S. Weir ed., *The Gonds of Central India*, London, 1973, no.126.

71

Central Indian brasses from the Luard collection. Madhya Pradesh, 18th–19th century

Gift of Mrs. Luard, 1936; formerly collection of Col. C.E. Luard

These seven objects belonged to a large collection of brass images, ritual objects, implements, ornaments and toys which was formed by Major (later Colonel) C. Eckford Luard in the former Central India Agency between 1900 and 1903. Luard served in this area for a number of years as Superintendent of Gazetteer and of Census Operations. He compiled the several volumes of *Central Indian State Gazetteers* (1907–12), as well as writing other works, including guide-books to Dhar and Mandu and the Dilwara temples at Mount Abu. In later life he lived at Boar's Hill, Oxford, and part of his collection was presented to the Indian Institute's museum by his widow in 1936 (see also no.57). Luard's earlier article describing the collection in the *Journal of Indian Art and Industry* is still useful in the identification of regional types of such late brass objects, which are otherwise scantily documented.

Images of gods, as might be expected, formed the larger part of Luard's collection. Some, like the figure of Durgā killing the buffalo-demon (71a), adhere

a. Durgā Mahiṣāsuramardinī
Height $5\frac{1}{2}$ in. (13.9 cm.)
X.280

c. Cover for a *liṅga*
Height $14\frac{3}{4}$ in. (37.5 cm.)
X.292

b. Śiva and Pārvatī
Height $5\frac{7}{8}$ in. (14.8 cm.)
X.283

d. Stand for a *liṅga* with cobra
Height $18\frac{1}{2}$ in. (47 cm.)
X.287

e. Temple lamp
Height 11 in. (28 cm.)
X.284

f. Incense holder in the form of a woman
Height 7 in. (17.8 cm.)
X.279

g. Incense holder in the form of Garuḍa
Height 9 in. (22.8 cm.)
X.281

loosely to classical canons of iconography (see no. 31), while others are in a more *janglī* (rustic) idiom, such as a seated group of Śiva and Pārvatī with a stylised Nandī at their feet (71b).

One of the most interesting and unusual objects is the large, hollow *liṅga* cover (71c), which would have been placed over the stone emblem of the god in a Śiva temple: a very similar example can be seen *in situ* in the Udayeśvara temple at Udayapur (Madhya Pradesh) in a published photograph (Daniélou, *loc. cit.*). The cover itself bears the face of Śiva, in the manner of an *ekamukhaliṅga*. It has eyelets at the side for attaching chains. The copper top may be a later replacement. Luard notes, "... the screw in front must have once borne a figure of Gaṅgā. This is a very rare piece, such specimens being seldom obtained . . .". Comparable *liṅga* covers, with heroic or martial faces, are found in Maharashtra and Karnataka (Jayakar, *loc. cit.*).

Another striking Śaivite object is the cobra stand for a *bāṇaliṅga* (71d), the name given to the smooth, egg-shaped, white quartz stones found in the Narmada river-bed, which are collected and worshipped as *liṅgas*. The stand (now vacant) is protected by the snake with spread hood and protruding fangs. Its two upper sections are detachable.

Among the ritual objects from the collection is a massively sturdy, chalice-shaped temple lamp with a serrated rim (71e), which is said to have come from a Śaiva shrine. Around the cup section appear four figures in high relief, of Gaṇeśa; Hanumān; Bhairava (a fierce aspect of Śiva) with his dog, holding in his hands a drum, a sword, a cup full of blood and a severed head; and the Goddess, carrying in her hands the mace and discus of Viṣṇu and the trident and sword of Śiva; a pair of *pāduka* (foot-marks of Viṣṇu) also appear, with the sun and moon above them.

A more elegant and harmoniously modelled *pūjā* accessory is a female attendant figure (71f), standing with legs crossed, her extended hand enclosing a holder for an incense-stick (*agarbatti*). She wears only jewellery above the waist and has a thick plait of hair hanging down at the back. Another incense-holder is in the form of Viṣṇu's vehicle, the celestial bird Garuḍa (71g), represented as a beak-nosed bird-man kneeling in the gesture of adoration or salutation (*añjali-mudrā*). Flame-like wings and hanging drapes (damaged at the right side) emanate from his upper arms. A snake (*nāga*) – traditionally Garuḍa's enemy and his chief food – rests docilely in front of him. On the tubular *agarbatti*-holder rising from his crown the name of the god Rām appears in relief.

PUBLISHED

Major C.E. Luard, "A collection of brass from Central India", *Journal of Indian Art and Industry*, XVI, 1914 pp.114–16, pls.10–12; see also A. Daniélou, *Hindu Polytheism*, London, 1964, pl.19; P. Jayakar, *The Earthen Drum*, New Delhi, 1980, pp.189–90.

72
Equestrian figure, bronze, hollow cast. Rajasthan or Central India, 19th century

Height $7\frac{1}{2}$ in. (19 cm.)
1964.160
Gift of Mr. H.L. Dunkley

Folk bronzes of horsemen were produced in great numbers in Western and Central India, where the cults flourished of various deified heroes who were represented as mounted Rajput warriors. Among the aboriginal Bhil tribes, a bronze figurine of a horseman, or Spirit Rider, also played a central part in the rites performed at death to help the departed spirit in its ascent to the world beyond, the metal figure becoming the spirit's temporary abode (Kramrisch, *loc. cit.*). The Bhils likewise represented their ancestors as horsemen in their memorial stones, although they, like the common people of India generally, did not themselves possess or use horses, which were the prized prerogative of the Rajput aristocracy.

Elevated on elongated, tapering legs, the plumed and caparisoned horse and its slant-eyed, martial rider have an imposing and barbarous presence. The latter holds the reins and the hilt of his sheathed sword; he also wears a *katar*, curved dagger and a bossed shield at his back. The conventional royal umbrella (*chattra*) above his conical head-dress may derive from the iconography of the minor solar deity Revanta, a son of Sūrya, who was represented as a mounted nobleman with ceremonial umbrella and was worshipped as a saviour from the dangers of the forest. The projections below three of the horse's feet may once have been inserted into cross-bars with attached wheels, and the figurine could have thus been used as a toy.

LITERATURE

S. Kramrisch, *Unknown India: Ritual art in tribe and village*, Philadelphia, 1968, pp.52–56, pls.XI–XVI; B.N. Sharma, *The Iconography of Revanta*, New Delhi, 1975.

73
Brass *cambū*. Benares, 18th century

Height $7\frac{1}{4}$ in. (18.5 cm.) Diameter 6 in. (15 cm.)
X.2103

In India even the plainest brass or copper domestic utensils have always been made with a remarkable beauty and variety of form. The *loṭa*, a globular or melon-shaped water-vessel with a reflexed rim by which it is carried, is one of the most common types, being universally used by Hindus for ablutions and other purposes (Muslims generally used spouted ewers, to provide the freely running water required by religious law for their ablutions). More elaborately decorated vessels such as this brass *cambū*, which differs from a *loṭa* in its narrower neck and short conical foot, were made for use in religious ceremonies. It is of a type associated with the holy city of Benares (Varanasi, or Kāśī) on the bank of the Ganges, the abode of Śiva and a major pilgrimage centre for countless centuries. The content of the several bands of incised decoration around the body of the *cambū* suggests that it was made for a Vaiṣṇava rather than a Śaiva worshipper. Similar vessels which have been found in various parts of India were probably sent from Benares as containers for Ganges water.

The *cambū* is of near-spherical shape, rising to a pointed apex and everted lip with lotus petal decoration; the interior of the base is missing. Of the five principal registers of decoration, the uppermost depicts eight figures of Kṛṣṇa and the milkmaids dancing with linked hands in the *rāsamaṇḍala* circle. Further below is an inscribed band with a thrice-repeated invocation to Rāma (*śrī rām nām jaya rām nām*). Beneath this are two broader central registers. The higher of these comprises eight scenes of the exploits of Kṛṣṇa, including the theft of the milkmaids' clothes, the raising of Mount Govardhana, the subduing of the snake-king Kāliya and the slaying of the evil king Kaṁsa; the lower has twelve scenes, showing Gaṇeśa, Śiva seated on the bull Nandī with the Ganges river issuing from his hair, and the ten *avatāras* of Viṣṇu, ranged clock-wise round the bowl (the Jagannātha trio appears as the ninth *avatāra*, between Kṛṣṇa and Kalki). The Ganges stream pouring downwards from Śiva's head traverses the next band of decoration, which consists of schematic scenes representing the temples and sacred sites on the Panchakroshi road. This famous route encircling Benares is followed by pilgrims circumambulating the holy city to expiate their sins; the journey normally takes five days and includes visits to 108 shrines along the way. Various deities presiding in the main temples are here depicted, interspersed with several *liṅga* shrines, a Nandī, a *Viṣṇupada* (footprint of Viṣṇu), groups of religious vessels(?), a temple tank with pillars at the corners, a sun symbol and a conventional tree or plant (reported by Mrs. Rivett Carnac as representing the gram plant, an important source of food). The stream from Śiva's

locks then enters the lowest band encircling the base of the *cambū*, which represents the sacred Ganges river itself. In it are depicted a primordial tortoise (*Kūrma avatāra?*) guarding the point of inflow, four large fish, an empty boat with four oars, six conch shells and a large snake.

A comparable *cambū* in the Victoria and Albert Museum (I.S. 464-1883), with a slightly more compressed body shape and a less worn decorative surface, is inscribed with a date V.S. 1822/1765–66 A.D.

LITERATURE
M. Rivett Carnac, "Copper Chambu or Sacrificial Vessel from Benares", *Journal of Indian Art and Industry*, I, 10, 1886, pp.72–76.

74
Toy soldiers, brass. Vizagapatam district, late 18th century

Height ranging from $9\frac{1}{16}$ in. (23 cm.) to $3\frac{5}{8}$ in. (9.2 cm.)
1969.44 (a–g); 1975.26; 1977.10 (a–d)
Given by Mr. A.J. Prior and Mr. S. Digby

These small brass figures are most unusual in Indian sculpture for their skilful and charming representation, bordering on humorous caricature, of contemporary military types. The seven mounted figures in the Ashmolean's group comprise a mustachioed officer on an elephant, a similarly mustachioed lancer on a frisky horse, a matchlock-man on a capering camel, a negro carabineer, a rocket-man with two tall rocket-launchers, a cavalier with a curved sword and a horse and rider in a quilted cap and coats. There are also four footsoldiers, smaller in scale and less elaborately finished, which may be of a later date. These comprise a European infantryman in a tricorne hat, a native sepoy of the East India Company's Madras Army and two Indian spearmen. Other groups of Vizagapatam figures are in the Madras Museum, the Madras School of Art, the Victoria and Albert Museum, the National Army Museum, the Royal collection at Sandringham and private collections. With their large heads, squat bodies, enormous weapons and upright bearing, they "graphically illustrate the whole gamut of military swagger in man and beast" (Birdwood).

Their traditional attribution to Vizagapatam (Vishakhapatnam) on India's eastern coast is supported by the unique inscriptions on the Ashmolean's elephant figure, giving the date 1795 on its forehead and the name Vizagapatam in Roman capitals on its rump. A Company factory (or trading-post) had been established there in the late 17th century, and in 1794 the British took over control from the debt-ridden local Raja. The administrative officials who then moved in may have been among the first European collectors of the brass soldiers, which were possibly first manufactured for a local ruler, albeit after European models, for the style and characterisation of the figures, as well as their solid rectangular bases, are quite un-Indian.

Thurston records two traditions describing their origin at Peddapuram, a town about 80 miles south of Vizagapatam and at that time the capital of a large *zamīndārī* estate. According to one story, the local Raja, Timma Razu (d. 1797), had the figures made on the advice of his astrologer for presentation to Brahmins in order to avert his threatened death. Another version has the astrologer suggesting that for the Raja to hold a review of the toy army each day, without blood being shed, would have the same desirable effect. The names of the artist and the two craftsmen concerned were recorded as Adimurti and the brothers Virachandracharlu and Viracharlu respectively, and the whole army of figures was said to have been sold off at the beginning of the 19th century. However this may be, some evidence for the popularity of such toy armies with the Deccani minor nobility of the time is provided by a painting in the State Museum, Hyderabad, in which a Raja sits listening to music on a garden terrace while a procession of toy soldiers parades along the path in front of him (Zebrowski, *loc. cit.*). Such model armies must have been cheaper and more manageable than the real thing.

The production of toy-soldiers was itself a European fashion dating from the Renaissance period. Armies made of precious metals were especially popular at the French court in the 17th century, but these were all later melted down and, even in base metals, very few early examples now survive. In England solid toy-soldiers ("solids", as apposed to "flats" or two-dimensional examples) appear to have been unknown until after the Napoleonic wars, and it is therefore likely that the Vizagapatam soldiers are the oldest large group of "solids" to have survived. Unlike Western examples, they are not manufactured uniformly by piece-moulding, but are individually modelled and cast by the *cire perdue* process, thus allowing a greater variety of detail and expression. The question of their evident debt to a European source remains an interesting problem. It is perhaps likely that the prototypes were modelled not by Thurston's shadowy "Ādimūrti", a Sanskrit (Brahmin?) name meaning "primordial image", but by a talented European amateur artist, with an eye for caricature, in the English or French military service.

PUBLISHED

J.C. Harle, "Toy soldiers", *The Oxford Magazine*, 6 February 1970, pp.136–39; S. Digby and J.C. Harle, *Toy Soldiers and Ceremonial in post-Mughal India*, Oxford, 1982, pp.5–7 and pls.; also: G. Birdwood, *The Industrial Arts of India*, London, 1880, p.162, pls.20–26; E. Thurston, "Brass manufacture in the Madras Presidency", *Journal of Indian Art and Industry*, IV, no.34, April 1891, pp.9–10, pl.29; Sir G. Birdwood, "The collections of Indian Art in Marlborough House and at Sandringham Hall", *Journal of Indian Art and Industry*, IV, no.37, Jan. 1892, p.27, pls.64, 65; E. Thurston et al., *Illustrations of Metal Work in Brass and Copper mostly South Indian*, Madras, 1913, figs.95–101; Sotheby's sale cat., 24 November 1986, lot 264.

LITERATURE

M. Zebrowski, *Deccani Painting*, London, 1983, fig.258.

75

The Cavalcade of the King of Oudh, bronze figures, bolted to a bronze base. Oudh, c.1820

$7\frac{1}{2} \times 15\frac{1}{2} \times 9\frac{1}{2}$ in. (19.1 × 39.4 × 24.1 cm.)
1977.25

This unusually ambitious royal procession scene is both a masterpiece of folk bronze-casting and an eloquent commentary on the meeting of Indian and European cultures in the post-Mughal period. Riding in one of the elephant howdahs is the King of Oudh, probably Ghāzī ud-Dīn Haidar (r.1814–27), wearing a tall, pointed crown, with his chief minister beside him. In the adjacent howdah sit the British Resident at Lucknow, wearing a crescent-shaped chapeau-bras, and his assistant in a shovel hat. They are accompanied by the two mahouts with elephant goads and an attendant (another is missing from the King's howdah), with an escort of eight *sawārs* (horsemen) riding in front and behind them and twelve *sipāhīs* (sepoys, or foot-soldiers) in two lines flanking the group. The latter are dressed in the uniform of the East India Company's army or an Oudh version of it.

The Nawab Wazirs of Oudh (or Avadh), who were of Persian origin, had risen to prominence at the Mughal court of Delhi before establishing themselves in the mid-18th century as virtually autonomous rulers with their capital at Lucknow. Here they indulged in ostentatious display and lavish artistic patronage in the traditional Mughal manner. A number of Europeans were attracted to their court, including the painters Zoffany and Tilly Kettle in the 1770s and '80s. As the East India Company strengthened its control over northern India and the Nawabs became virtual puppets, the European taste in architecture and decoration was increasingly emulated at Lucknow, with florid and fantastic results. Ghāzī ud-Dīn, who had assumed the title of King bestowed on him by George III in 1819, encouraged this exuberant eclecticism. He appointed as his court artist the Scottish painter Robert Home, who produced not only pictures but countless designs for the monarch's royal trappings, including crowns, regalia, costumes, uniforms, carriages and exotically shaped thrones and boats; Ghāzī ud-Dīn's favourite crown was the spiky, Christmas-cracker model seen here.

According to the protocol agreed under the 1819 treaty, the British Resident and the King were to be treated as equals on ceremonial occasions. Here the two ride side by side in procession, the swaying motion of their elephants suggested by the tilt of the howdahs. All of the figures are modelled in an individual and animated manner. Those in the howdahs turn towards each other in conversation. Two of the leading horses rear dramatically on their hind-legs. The sepoys march in less than perfect drill order, gazing this way and that. The raffish pomp of the occasion is well caught. It is likely that the complex composition follows a European design and is the work of a craftsman trained in producing religious images and toy figures.

PUBLISHED

S. Digby and J.C. Harle, *Toy Soldiers and Ceremonial in post-Mughal India*, Oxford, 1982, pp.8–10; S.C. Welch, *India: Art and Culture 1300–1900*, Exhib. Cat., New York, 1985, no.283.

76

Hair-dressing scene, terracotta, painted with black on a white mica ground. Murshidabad district, Bengal, early 20th century

Height $4\frac{1}{2}$ in. (11.5 cm.) Length 5 in. (12.7 cm.)
X.2297

The Museum has a number of figurines and toys in painted wood and terracotta from Bengal, Orissa, Rajasthan and other regions. Ephemeral by nature and therefore relatively recent in date, they nevertheless embody ancient traditions of modelling and decoration answering to the timeless needs and way of life of rural communities. Whether for use as temporary images in domestic religious rituals, as household utensils or as children's playthings, they are produced with a lively dexterity and spontaneity of execution according to long established conventions.

This hair-dressing scene of two kneeling women with raised heads and curving, elongated arms is described as coming from Katalia, Murshidabad district. It is of a type popular in West Bengal, said by Mookerjee to be "commonly known as Birbhum toys because they are sold at the Paus-mela [fair] at Santiniketan". The figures are freely modelled by hand but a mould has been used for the faces. A silvery-white mica coating is applied overall, finished with strokes of black colour defining the hair, eyes and jewellery.

LITERATURE

A. Mookerjee, *Folk Toys of India*, Calcutta, 1956, pl.9, p.22; M.K. Pal, *Catalogue of Folk Art in the Asutosh Museum*, Calcutta, 1962, p.18, pl.VIII, fig.12; Whitechapel Art Gallery, *Arts of Bengal*, London, 1979, no.158.

77

COLOUR PLATE 10

Portable Viṣṇu shrine, wood and cloth, painted and lacquered, with other materials. Tirupati, South India, late 18th or early 19th century

Height $16\frac{1}{2}$ in. (41 cm.) greatest Width 12 in. (30.5 cm.), greatest Depth $4\frac{3}{4}$ in. (12 cm.)
X.264
Given by the Church Missionary Society

Tirupati, where this small shrine was made, is an important Vaiṣṇava pilgrimage town to the north-west of Madras, now in the state of Andhra Pradesh. The Abbé Dubois, a missionary working in South India in the early 19th century, described the teeming life of its temple, which "is dedicated to Vishnu under the name of Venkateswara. Immense multitudes of pilgrims flock to it from all parts of India, bringing offerings of all sorts, in food, stuffs, gold, silver, jewels, costly cloths, horses, cows, &c., which are so considerable that they suffice to maintain several thousands of persons employed in the various offices of worship, which is there conducted with extraordinary magnificence."

It is believed that portable shrines of this type, with multiple doors and folding panels densely painted with mythological scenes, were used by itinerant priests who sang or narrated the sacred stories of Viṣṇu and his incarnations to village audiences. The two outer doors and their lacquered cloth flap extensions are painted (on the outer side) with scenes of Viṣṇu reclining on the snake Ananta, episodes from the childhood of Kṛṣṇa and the *Rāmāyaṇa* and various

figures of deities. On the inner sides appear Rāma enthroned and standing figures of Viṣṇu in various forms, including Veṅkateśa (as worshipped at Tirupati), Raṅganātha (as worshipped at Śrirangam) and Varadarājā (as worshipped at Kanchipuram). The narrow inner doors have figures of the avatars of Viṣṇu on the outside and deities, devotees and others on the inside. The flimsy innermost doors, with numerous rectangular mica windows, open to reveal the painted wooden image of Viṣṇu standing with *cakra* and *śaṅkha* in his upper hands, the lower hands in *varada-mudrā* and resting on his thigh; a sword rests against his other thigh. The figure is profusely encrusted with metallic and glass "jewellery". To the right are smaller standing figures of Rāma and Kṛṣṇa and, above them, Viṣṇu (?) beneath a snake-hood. The back and sides of the shrine are painted a deep blue with flowering tree designs within engrailed arches. The quality of the painted decoration is crisp and vigorous throughout.

The preservation of the few surviving examples of these shrines is in part due to Christian missionaries working in South India who sent them to Europe as documents of Hindu religious practice. The earliest such example, now in Halle (East Germany) was sent from Madras by the missionary Sartorius in 1733; another is in the Museo Missionario Etnologico in the Vatican. The present shrine was similarly collected by the Church Missionary Society. Another (of unknown provenance) is in the Museum für Völkerkunde, Munich.

LITERATURE

R.M. Cimino, "Il 'sacellum indicum n.1' dell' antico Museo Borgia di Velletri", *Rivista degli Studi Orientali*, LI, 1977, pp.141–62; C. Mallebrein, *Skulpturen aus Indien: Bedeutung und Form*, Munich, Staatliches Museum für Völkerkunde, 1984, pp.209–25; L. Icke-Schwalbe, "Betrachtungen zur volkstümlichen Hindukunst in Südostindien", *Abhandlungen und Berichte des Staatlichen Museums für Völkerkunde, Dresden*, Bd.31, 1970, pp.1–24; J. Appasamy, *Tanjavur Painting of the Maratha Period*, New Delhi, 1980, pp.78–79, pls.28–29; Abbé J.A. Dubois, *Hindu Manners, Customs and Ceremonies*, 3rd ed., Oxford, 1906, pp.601–2.

78

Temple-hanging, cotton, painted and dyed. Kalahasti region, Madras state c.1880–90

Height 7 ft. 4 in. (224 cm.) Width 10 ft. 11 in. (333 cm.)
X.2067

Temple-hangings of this type had a didactic purpose, surrounding the central panel showing the deity with numerous mythological narrative scenes arranged in compartmented registers in the manner of a cartoon strip. Their stylistic conventions followed local traditions of temple mural-painting, which in the far south were untouched by Mughal influences from northern India. The outlines were stencilled on the cotton ground and then freely painted by hand with dye-colours; the mordant-dyeing process was also used for some colours. In this hanging the central panel depicts the god Rāma enthroned with his wife Sītā and attended by his three brothers, under an arching canopy supporting three *gopura* (temple towers) and celestial figures. Scenes from the *Rāmāyaṇa* epic occupy eight registers, divided by narrow bands inscribed with Telugu commentary. The overall effect is sombrely rich and eventful, even though the pictorial forms had become stereotyped by the late 19th century. A comparable example is in the Victoria and Albert Museum (1.S.75-1886, purchased from the 1886 Colonial and Indian Exhibition; see Jayakar and Irwin) and a more modern version is in the Calico Museum of Textiles, Ahmedabad (see Irwin and Hall).

LITERATURE
P. Jayakar and J. Irwin, *Textiles and Ornaments of India*, New York, 1956, pp.60–61; J. Irwin and M. Hall, *Indian Painted and Printed Fabrics*, Ahmedabad, 1971, pp.66–67, 78–79, pl.43.

79 COLOUR PLATE II

The Jagannātha Trio, painted and lacquered wood. Puri, Orissa, c.1900 (?)

$9\frac{1}{4} \times 14$ in. (23.5×35.6 cm.)
X.2282

Kṛṣṇa is worshipped in various forms in different regions of India, for example as Śrī Nāthjī at the shrine of Nathdwara in Rajasthan (see no.106b) and as Jagannātha, "Lord of the World", at Puri in Orissa. The temple shrine at Puri houses a family trio of primitive, wooden post-like images with painted faces, comprising Jagannātha, with a black face and round eyes, his brother Balabhadra, with a white face and oval eyes, and the shorter figure of their sister, Subhadrā; a fourth image, standing for the Sudarśana Cakra or Wheel of Viṣṇu, stands apart from the group. The crude simplicity of these images suggests that they are a survival of an earlier local cult which became absorbed by Vaiṣṇavism. The gods are attended by numerous temple staff, who treat them in the customary way like human princes, bathing, clothing and feeding them at regular times during the day. Pilgrims have gathered at Puri for centuries, and the huge temple cars in which Jagannātha and his companions are pulled in procession at the Rath Jatra festival gave rise to the English word "juggernaut".

Paintings of Jagannātha, most commonly shown with Balabhadra and Subhadrā, have long been sold in great numbers around the temple to devotees attending the many annual festivals. Like the Kalighat paintings of Calcutta (no.80) they were painted rapidly, usually on cloth or paper, and sold cheaply. The economy of technique and simple, earthy colouring of this image of the goggle-eyed triad, draped in garlands and with their stumpy arms held aloft, serve to convey a sense of their spiritual power in the eyes of their worshippers.

LITERATURE
M. Archer, *Indian Popular Painting in the India Office Library*, London, 1977, pp.105 et seq.

80 COLOUR PLATE 12
Hanumān, water-colour with silver on paper. Kalighat, Calcutta, c.1870.

50 × 37½ in. (125 × 96 cm.)
1966.183

The work of the *patua* artists of eastern India, who produced narrative scrolls illustrating the religious epics for use by itinerant picture-showmen, was among the most vital forms of Indian folk painting in the 18th and 19th centuries, and probably much earlier. The Kalighat style is a distinctive urban variant of this ancient tradition. The Kālī temple which was built in 1809 at Kalighat, now in the southern suburbs of Calcutta, had quickly become a major pilgrimage centre. Shops and stalls near the temple made a brisk trade selling wood and clay dolls and images and brightly coloured paintings of the gods to visiting pilgrims. As the paintings were made to sell as cheaply as possible, they show a steadily increasing rapidity of execution. The flowing outlines of the figures were boldly accentuated by dark areas of wash in imitation of European modelling. The artists' subject matter included not only gods and goddesses but satirical studies of modern, Westernised fashions and famous scandals of the day. In the later 19th century their work declined in the face of competition from mass-produced woodcuts and finally from the garish chromolithographic prints which are still found all over India today.

This painting of the monkey-god Hanumān, the helper of Rāma and Sītā in the *Rāmāyaṇa* and one of the most popular of Indian deities, is striking for its unusual size, equivalent to eight normal sheets of the paper used by Kalighat painters. It was possibly made as a special order for a European customer, as it formerly belonged to the London Missionary Society, for whom it may have served as a lecturing aid. (A similar painting from the same source in the Museum's collection depicts Śiva as Ascetic and Musician.) Hanumān's face, hands, feet and necklace are highlighted in silver and his body is pale blue, the paint streaked to represent fur; the background is yellow. The iconography is slightly unusual, as in this kneeling posture Hanumān is more often shown with hands raised to his chest, displaying the diminutive figures of Rāma and Sītā enshrined in his heart.

LITERATURE
W.G. Archer, *Kalighat Painting*, London, 1971.

81
Pābūjī's *paṛ*, painting on cloth, used as a portable temple for the folk-god Pābūjī. Bhilwara, south-east Rajasthan, 1983. Painted by Nandkishor Joshi for the *bhopā* Chotuji

Height 58 in. (147 cm.) Length 202 in. (515 cm.)
1985.20

This long cloth-painting (*paṛ*), profusely filled with narrative scenes according to a long established iconography, is in function a portable temple of the Rajasthani folk-god Pābūjī. Such paintings are carried from village to village by travelling folk-priests (*bhopās*), who unroll and erect them as a backdrop to their night-long recitations of the Pābūjī epic, with musical accompaniment usually provided by their wives. Such shows were familiar to Colonel Tod in the early 19th century, who writes in his *Annals and antiquities of Rajasthan* of "the itinerant bard and showman, who annually goes his round, exhibiting in pictorial delineations, while he recites in rhyme, the deeds of this warrior [Pābūjī] to the gossiping villagers of the desert".

Very few of the *paṛs* which survive are of any great age; the earliest, in honour of another folk-god,

Devnarāyaṇ, is dated 1867 A.D. The Museum's example was painted by Nandkishor (born 1954), one of the younger artists at Bhilwara at the present day, who was trained by his father Dhanraj and his grandfather Kalyanmal, members of the Joshi clan of the Chipa caste (hereditarily associated with cloth-painting). Although brasher in colouring and more mechanical in line than the work of previous generations of artists, it is nonetheless a skilful and authentic example of the *paṛ* tradition.

(detail)

THE MUGHAL AND BRITISH PERIODS

82 COLOUR PLATE 13

Amīr Hamza overthrows 'Amr-i Ma'dī Kariba; an illustration to the *Dāstān-i Amīr Hamza*, gouache on cloth. Mughal, c.1562–65

$26\frac{1}{4} \times 19\frac{1}{2}$ in. (67 × 49.5 cm.)
1978.2596
Given by Mr. Gerald Reitlinger

Akbar, the third and greatest of the Mughal emperors (r.1556–1605), was a ruler of unusual vision and restless energy. Inheriting the throne at the age of fourteen, he extended Mughal power throughout northern India, while taking a keen and tolerant interest in the religions and customs of his subject peoples. As a patron, he brought together a large atelier of native artists, many of them Hindus, under the direction of the Persian masters, Mīr Sayyid 'Alī and 'Abd us-Samad, whom his father Humayūn had earlier brought back to India from his exile at the Persian court. Under Akbar's close supervision a dynamic style of manuscript illustration was formed, combining Persian elegance of line and decoration with the robuster vitality of Indian painting and further naturalistic elements deriving from European art which had begun to reach the Mughal court. The main forcing-ground for this rapid stylistic synthesis was the illustrated series of the *Dastān-i Amīr Hamza* (or *Hamza-nāma*), a rambling epic narrative, describing the fantastic adventures of its hero Hamza, which appealed greatly to the young Akbar. A chronicler tells us that on one occasion in 1564 (about the time that the Ashmolean page may have been illustrated) he amused himself after an elephant hunt by listening to its stories; and a later historian relates that he would even recite them himself in his harem in the manner of a traditional story-teller.

The illustrated series originally comprised 1400 large paintings on cotton cloth, bound in fourteen volumes. This uniquely ambitious project occupied the imperial studio for about fifteen years (c.1562–77). The earliest illustrations, such as the present one, were produced under Mīr Sayyid 'Alī's direction and are often noticeably Persian in feeling. In many cases they also have the (paper) text panels on the painted side rather than the reverse, as became usual later. The subject here is an early episode in the epic, in which the youthful hero Hamza, encountering the gigantic warrior 'Amr-i Ma'dī Kariba on the battlefield, topples both horse and rider with a mere thrust of his foot (subsequently 'Amr-i Ma'dī is converted to Islam and becomes one of Hamza's staunch helpers). Instead of the explicit carnage seen in some of the later pictures of the series, this scene of combat has an element of comic bathos. While the corpulent warrior sprawls headlong, arrows spilling from his quiver, many of the onlookers 'bite the finger of astonishment' in the Persian manner. The setting of the composition against a high rocky skyline with a stylised tree also adheres closely to the Persian pictorial tradition, though the spirited figures of trumpeters and percussionists above the horizon are more typically Indian.

At some point after the mid-18th century the 1400 pages of the *Dāstān-i Amīr Hamza* were dispersed from the imperial library, and rather more than a tenth of them are now known to survive. Another page, showing Hamza burning the wooden chest of

Zoroaster (Glück, fig.47), has recently been placed on loan to the Museum.

PUBLISHED

H. Glück, *Die indischen Miniaturen des Haemzae – Romanes*, Vienna, 1925, p.28, fig.2.

83

While the sage Uttaṅka is in the river, the snake king Takṣaka steals the ear-rings; from a dispersed manuscript of the *Razm-nāma*, Gouache on paper. Mughal, 1598. By Āsa

8 × 4 in. (20 × 10.5 cm.)
1978.2591
Given by Mr. Gerald Reitlinger

As part of his plan to promote understanding between his Muslim and Hindu subjects, Akbar ordered that several Hindu texts, including the *Mahābhārata* and the *Rāmāyaṇa*, should be made available in Persian translation. Magnificent illustrated copies of each of the two epics were made for the imperial library and these are now in the Jaipur royal collection. Less splendid versions were copied and illustrated for the Mughal nobility, though few examples now survive. It has been suggested that the patron of the 1598 *Razm-nāma* manuscript could have been 'Abd ur-Rahīm Khānkhānān, Akbar's leading minister and a famous bibliophile who employed his own artists. However it is more likely that the manuscript, though not of full imperial quality and possibly destined for a nobleman's library, was in fact produced in Akbar's studio by younger apprentice artists, many of them the sons of established painters.

The scene illustrated here is an early episode from the first book of the *Mahābhārata*, in which, while the young sage Uttaṅka is fetching water, the snake-king Takṣaka steals the ear-rings which had been given to Uttaṅka by Pauṣya's queen. It is painted in the mature Akbari style, a synthesis of Persian, Indian and (especially in the landscape) European elements, but the colouring, with dominant grey and khaki tones, is untypically muted. Āsa (or Āsi), son of Maheṣa, painted nine pages of this *Razm-nāma* and is known to have worked on several other manuscripts of the period.

The manuscript was largely dispersed at auction in 1921. Five other pages are in the Museum's collection, also the gift of Gerald Reitlinger.

PUBLISHED

Ashmolean Museum, *Eastern Ceramics and other Works of Art from the Collection of Gerald Reitlinger*, Oxford, 1981, no.404; J. Seyller, "Model and Copy: The Illustration of Three *Razm-nāma* Manuscripts", *Archives of Asian Art*, XXXVIII, 1985, p.56.

84

St. John the Evangelist (After Dürer), brush drawing, with light tinting. By Abū'l Hasan. Mughal, dated 1600

Height 4 in. Width $1\frac{3}{4}$ in. (10 × 4.6 cm.)
1978.2597
Given by Mr. Gerald Reitlinger
Inscribed: *Shāh Salīm; mashqahu abū'l ḥasan ibn rizā murīd dar sinn-i sīzdah salagī sākhta batārīkh yazdahum shahr-i rabī' al ākhir sana 1009 rūz-i jumi' ṣūrat itimām yāft*

This small and unusually expressive rendering of the figure of St. John from the engraving of the Crucifixion in Albrecht Dürer's Passion series of 1500 is the earliest known work by Abū'l Hasan, one of the most favoured artists of the emperor Jahāngīr (r.1605–27). An even keener connoisseur of painting than his

father Akbar, Jahāngīr admired above all Abū'l Hasan's brilliantly naturalistic technique and the sympathetic insight of his portraiture. In 1618 he wrote of the artist, "at the present time he has no rival or equal", and he bestowed on him the title "Wonder of the Age".

The son of the distinguished Persian painter Āqā Rizā, Abū'l Hasan had grown up in the service of Prince Salīm (the future Jahāngīr). This drawing was executed in October 1600, when Salīm was already in revolt against the ageing Akbar and, as the Persian inscription tells us, Abū'l Hasan himself was only twelve years old (in his "thirteenth year"). The copying of European prints played an important part in the training of Mughal artists at this time. But Abū'l Hasan's dextrous reinterpretation of the figure of the Evangelist is more than a technical exercise. Mr. Robert Skelton has recently written of it, ". . . for a copy, particularly from one medium into another, it is a remarkable achievement. Working with a more subtle instrument than the graver's burin, the young Indian has substituted for Dürer's accomplished rendition of conventional saintly grief, a troubled expression of inner disquiet, which is all the more exceptional in that introspection of this sort is totally foreign to either Indian or Iranian art."

PUBLISHED

E. Wellesz, "Mughal Paintings at Burlington House", *Burlington Magazine*, XL, February 1948, fig.25; B. Gray, "Painting" in Sir L. Ashton ed., *The Art of India and Pakistan*, London, 1950, no.665, pl.128; British Museum, *Paintings from the Muslim Courts of India*, London, 1976, no.87; Ashmolean Museum, *Eastern Ceramics and other Works of Art from the Collection of Gerald Reitlinger*, London, 1981, no.408; see also M.C. Beach, *The Grand Mogul*, Williamstown, 1978, pp.86ff. and R. Skelton, "Europe and India", in *Europa und die Kunst des Islam, 15. bis 18. Jahrhundert*, XXV. Internationaler Kongress für Kunstgeschichte, Wien, 1983, Bd.5, pp.35–36.

85 COLOUR PLATE 14

'Abdullah Qutb Shah of Golconda, gouache with gold and silver on paper. Golconda, c.1640

Height 5 in. Width $3\frac{7}{8}$ in. (12.5 × 9.8 cm.)
1960.203

While the imperial Mughal style was developing in the late 16th and early 17th centuries, distinctive styles of painting had also evolved at the courts of the independent Muslim Sultans of the Deccan. Although they too derived from a synthesis of Persian and Indian styles, the Deccani schools differ greatly from the Mughal in character and mood. Where Mughal portraiture, for example, tends to a high degree of naturalism and a soberly official view of its empire-building subjects, the Deccani artists often produced charming and evocative informal portraits of their own, more hedonistic rulers, perhaps enjoying music, pleasant company or a siesta on a hot afternoon. They rendered these scenes with a refined and playful use of line and a subtle richness of colour.

From the 1630s, however, as the Mughal emperors steadily increased their political influence over the Deccan, their more formal conventions of portraiture were adopted and to some extent reinterpreted by the southern artists. In this painting Sultan 'Abdullah Qutb Shah of Golconda (1626–72) is shown seated in a dignified martial pose, holding the hilt of a sword in one hand and a kerchief in the other, on a low throne set on a garden terrace. The severe rectangular geometry of the composition contrasts with the brilliance of colouring of the ruler's flowered gold *jāma* and purple throne-seat, the pale blue of the cushion and scabbard, the pale green nimbus on a deeper green background. Above all, the sensitively modelled painting of the Sultan's thick-lipped features conveys a dreamy and abstracted quality, hinting at the true nature of this sensual and indolent ruler, whose administration was effectively controlled by his mother.

PUBLISHED

M. Zebrowski, *Deccani Painting*, London, 1983, p.183, fig.149.

86 COLOUR PLATE 15

Lovers by a lotus pool, gouache and gold on paper. Deccan or southern Rajasthan, c.1700

6.6 in. × 2.8 in. (16.7 × 7.1 cm.)
1983.129
Purchased with the aid of the Victoria & Albert Purchase Grant Fund, the Friends of the Ashmolean and the E.H. North Bequest

This simply conceived but delightful study of a noble couple embracing by a stream or pool with lotuses was probably painted around the beginning of the 18th century by a Rajasthani artist working under strong Deccani influences. During the 17th century many of the Rajput princes spent long periods campaigning with the Mughal armies in the Deccan and in some cases acquired a taste for the local styles of painting.

The picture is also of interest in that it has an unusually early English provenance (though not so early as the Indian album given by Archbishop Laud to the Bodleian Library in 1640). It bears marks showing that it belonged to three well known 18th century collectors of old master drawings, John Richardson senior (1665–1745), his son John Richardson junior and John Barnard (d.1784). The elder Richardson, who was himself an artist, is known to have owned a group of Rembrandt's drawings based on Mughal paintings, as well as an album of Indian drawings.

PUBLISHED

M.-C. David and J. Soustiel, *Miniatures Orientales de l'Inde*, 3, Paris, 1983, no.84; R. Skelton, "Indian Art and Artefacts in Early European collecting', in O. Impey and A. MacGregor eds., *The Origins of Museums*, Oxford, 1985, p.279, fig.107.

87

The *sakhī's* exhortation; an illustration to the *Amaru Śataka*, gouache on paper. Malwa, Central India, late 17th century

7 × 5 in. (17.6 × 13.5 cm.)
1979.13

During the 18th century a forceful style of illustrative painting flourished at the Hindu courts of the Malwa and Bundelkhand regions in Central India; very little inscriptional evidence has come to light that would help to distinguish its main local variants. Even more than contemporary work in Rajasthan to the west, the so-called Malwa style is a continuation of an indigenous, 16th century painting tradition, with less of the subsequent refining overlay of Mughal influence than elsewhere. It remains primitive and direct in form and colouring, sometimes tending to stiffness and repetitiveness. As at the other Rajput courts, the usual subject matter includes scenes from the religious epics, *rāgamālā* themes (see no.88) and, not least, poetical texts describing the emotions and behaviour of lovers, such as the Hindi *Rasikapriyā* of Keśava Dās and – more often illustrated in Central India than elsewhere – the Sanskrit verses of Amaru. This page from a series of the *Amaru-Śataka* (Hundred verses of Amaru) depicts a confidante (*sakhī*) remonstrating with a disconsolate heroine, who has been neglected by her unfaithful lover. Making an appropriate gesture, the *sakhī* exhorts her: "Women, wicked despite their loveliness, are stealing your only delight away and, though forbidden, they do not desist. Why do you suffer and weep in vain? Do them no such favours. Why not confront your beloved amorous tender-hearted young husband, my disheartened one, with a hundred loving, a hundred cruel harsh words and be your own best advocate?" The scene is set within a palace chamber, with a plain blue interior and a black sky which silhouettes a flying bird, a peacock on the palace roof and a plantain tree with its pendulous flower. The band of formalised scrollwork below is a common feature of these series.

LITERATURE

M. Chandra, "An Illustrated Set of the Amaru-Śataka", *Bulletin of the Prince of Wales Museum of Western India*, no.2, 1951–52, p.15, pl.I, fig.2.

88 COLOUR PLATE 16

Kamodanī *rāgiṇī*, gouache with silver and gold on paper. Bundi or Kotah, Rajasthan, c.1770

$8\frac{1}{4} \times 5$ in. (21 × 12.5 cm.); page size $14\frac{1}{4} \times 10\frac{1}{4}$ in. (36.3 × 25.5 cm.)
1958.148
Given by Lord Somervell

During the 17th and 18th centuries the local styles of painting at the semi-independent Rajput courts of Rajasthan, Central India and the Punjab Hills were stongly influenced by the imperial Mughal school. But in spite of the new popularity of portraiture, hunting scenes and other Mughal genres, the earlier tradition of poetical and devotional manuscript illustration also continued to flourish. The most common theme was *rāgamālā*, the representation of musical modes (*rāgas*) according to established iconographies described in poetical texts. With the Indian genius for theoretical classification, several of the main *rāgas* were endowed with families of "wives" (*rāgiṇīs*) and, in some systems, "sons" (*putras*) as well. Most *rāgamālās* comprise 36 *rāgas* and *rāgiṇīs*, but longer series are not uncommon. The conventional pictorial subjects are usually of ladies and princes seen in palaces or flowering groves, with a prevailing mood of erotic longing or fulfilment.

In this page Kamodanī *rāgiṇī* is depicted, according to a tradition followed at the neighbouring courts of Bundi and Kotah in south-east Rajasthan, as a lady preparing for a lover's tryst in a grove. According to the Sanskrit verses inscribed on the wide red border, she stretches out her lotus-like hand to collect the flowers, applies musk to her forehead, sits on a seat of

flowers and has "a soft and fair body. A young girl, like the *apsaras* Ra[ṁ]bha, dwelling in the heavenly realm, she is to be sung during the third watch of the day in the cold season, from the note Madhyama". It belongs to a *rāgamālā* of 36 pages which has been identified by Ebeling as a short version deriving from a huge series of 240 *rāga* pictures painted at Kotah in 1768, most of which are in the Sarasvatī Bhavan Library, Udaipur. Other pages from the present series are in the National Museum, New Delhi.

PUBLISHED

P. Rawson, *Indian Painting*, Paris, 1961, p.139; see also K. Ebeling, *Ragamala Painting*, Basel, 1973, p.220; E. and R.L. Waldschmidt, *Miniatures of Musical Inspiration*, vol.II, Berlin, 1975, pp.455, 292n.

89

The summer month of Jyeṣṭha, gouache on paper. Kotah, Rajasthan, c.1770

Height 10 in. (25 cm.) Width $6\frac{1}{2}$ in. (17 cm.)
1978.2568
Given by Mr. Gerald Reitlinger

The twelve months of the year (*bārahmāsa*) and their seasonal effects on the activities of idealised lovers were a popular theme of Hindi poets and of the painters at the Rajput courts who illustrated their evocative verses. This *bārahmāsa* page from Kotah depicts the scorching summer month of Jyeṣṭha (May–June), when the land is parched, the tanks are dry and neither man nor beast dare go out in the sun. Lovers should stay at home together in this season, and the *nāyaka* (hero, in the form of Kṛṣṇa) and his *nāyikā* (heroine) are shown taking their ease in Rajput fashion in the upper storey of a palace with a tall, balconied corner turret. The walls and roof are covered with cooling screens of dampened grass and two maids stand in attendance with a fan and punkah, while fountains play in the walled formal garden below. The *nāyikā* draws her lover's attention to the world outside, where men and animals are immobilised by the heat. Elephants and a tiger together seek the shade of a *pīpal* tree; a peacock and snake have forgotten their enmity and the deer stand unmolested by the hunters resting under another tree.

PUBLISHED

Ashmolean Museum, *Eastern Ceramics and Other Works of Art from the Collection of Gerald Reitlinger*, Oxford, 1981, no.411.

90 COLOUR PLATE 17

Mahārāṇa Bhīm Siṅgh with a hawk, gouache with gold on cloth. Udaipur, Rajasthan, c.1815–20. Attributed to Chokha

42 × 23 in. (107 × 59 cm.)
1985.31
Given by the Friends of the Ashmolean

During the second half of the 18th century the Rajput kingdoms suffered a general decline along with the central Mughal power, being ravaged repeatedly by Maratha invaders from the south. Peace and order were only restored when the Mahārājas accepted British protection in 1818. These decades of adversity encouraged a hedonistic tendency in the once formidable Rajput nobility. One such escapist was Mahārāṇā Bhīm Siṅgh, for fifty years the ruler of Mewar (1778–1828). Colonel Tod, who knew him well, writes in his *Annals and antiquities of Rajasthan*: ". . . though able, wise and amiable, his talents were nullified by numerous weak points. Vain shows, frivolous amusements, and an ill-regulated liberality alone occupied him . . .". Weak-willed and uninterested in administration, Bhīm Siṅgh fathered more than a hundred children. Intimate scenes of his private life as well as his public appearances were often painted by Chokha, one of the leading Mewar artists, whose squat, well-rounded and large-eyed figures are very distinctive. Most of Chokha's pictures are small scale works on paper; larger cloth-paintings such as this are generally rare in Rajasthani painting.

Although at first sight a conventional standing portrait of a ruler after the earlier Mughal manner, Chokha's depiction of his rotund and hairy-chested patron is unusually informal. Bhīm Siṅgh stands nonchalantly with one foot tucked behind the other – the bejewelled hawk on the royal finger also perches on one leg – with a flowered gold sash (*paṭka*) swathed round his ample hips. However, the Mahārāṇā's head is shown in full glory, the gold and green nimbus and crescent moon symbolising the divine ancestry of the Mewar rulers. The painting, which has suffered from water-staining at the left side, is inscribed with Bhīm Siṅgh's name and a valuation of 20 rupees (written on the side of the snub-nosed, Chokha-esque dog).

91 COLOUR PLATE 18

Bāz Bahādur and Rūpmatī, gouache with gold and silver on paper. Kulu, Punjab Hills, c.1720

$8\frac{1}{4} \times 10\frac{1}{8}$ in. (21 × 25.7 cm.)
1958.307
Given by Prof. R.C. Oldfield

The love of the 16th century Muslim prince Bāz Bahādur and his Hindu mistress Rūpmatī was a popular theme of poetry and song in Mughal India. During the 18th century the legendary couple were frequently depicted by artists at the provincial Mughal courts and at the Rajput courts of the Punjab Hills, especially Kulu and Garhwal. They are most often shown riding together, gazing into one another's eyes, either in the stillness of a moonlit night, or, as here, on a hawking expedition. Such romantic scenes had a strong appeal for the Muslim and Hindu nobility alike, for whom the convention of purdah allowed little association between the sexes.

Bāz Bahādur was the King of Malwa in Central India (1554–61) before its conquest by the armies of the emperor Akbar. A pleasure-loving and cultured prince, he was devoted to music and poetry and the company of singers and dancing-girls, his favourite being the celebrated beauty Rūpmatī. But in 1561 Bāz Bahādur was defeated by the Mughal general Adham Khān, and his harem along with his treasure and elephants fell into enemy hands. Soon after, Rūpmatī took poison to escape the lust of Adham Khān. After nine years as a fugitive, Bāz Bahādur submitted to

Akbar and joined the Mughal court, where he became famous for his skill as a singer.

In this painting the lovers' wild-eyed, mettlesome horses advance in step, while Rūpmatī turns in the saddle to gaze at the spellbound Bāz Bahādur. The figures are silhouetted against a cool grey ground, around which tightly drawn bushy trees cluster in pairs entwined with sinuous creepers. The conventional scene of the couple riding together is imbued with a certain eery tension often found in Kulu painting.

PUBLISHED

P. Rawson, *Indian Painting*, Paris, 1961, p.138; also W.G. Archer, *Indian Paintings from the Punjab Hills*, London, 1973, vol.1, p.335.

92

A commotion in the bazaar, gouache on paper. Guler, Punjab Hills, c.1750

8 × 11 in. (20.5 × 26.5 cm.)
1978.2595
Given by Mr. Gerald Reitlinger

Depictions of the daily life of the streets and bazaars are uncommon in Indian painting before the British period, only occasionally finding a place in the background of some mythological scene with an urban setting. This damaged but lively and enigmatic picture is an exception. It was painted in the Punjab Hills around the middle of the 18th century, when a fresh assimilation of the naturalistic elements of the

contemporary Mughal style followed the arrival of artists fleeing the uncertain political conditions of the Plains. It shows some elements of the style practised by Nainsukh, the best known member of a widely influential family of Pahari artists.

The artist's observation of gesture and attitude is keen and revealing. In the centre of the picture a miscreant is being beaten over the head with slippers by two armed officers, while in the foreground another is led away with hands tied and a slipper held humiliatingly over his head. As always in India, a small crowd gathers to watch the spectacle, while other figures go about their business. To the right, two boys choose sweets at a sweetshop. To the left, a husband buys a knife or jewellery from a display laid out on a cloth. In the foreground, two boys dance to the music of a *shehnai* and drum, while a Kānphaṭa yogī sits tranquilly before a *linga* shrine to the god Śiva.

PUBLISHED

Ashmolean Museum, *Eastern Ceramics and other Works of Art from the Collection of Gerald Reitlinger*, London, 1981, no.409; Victoria & Albert Museum, *The Indian Heritage: Court Life and Arts under Mughal Rule*, Exhib. Cat., London, 1982, no.161; *Petals from a Lotus*, Bradford, 1983, Cat. no.96.

93

Kṛṣṇa discards his garland; an illustration to the *Sat Saī* of Bihārī Lāl, gouache on paper. Garhwal, Punjab Hills, c.1800

$7\frac{3}{4} \times 5\frac{1}{2}$ in. (19.7 × 14.2 cm.); with border: $10\frac{1}{2} \times 8$ in. (26.5 × 20.5 cm.)

1967.164

A final flowering of Indian court painting took place in the Punjab Hills in the late 18th century. The renewed assimilation of Mughal pictorial conventions to the lyrical Rajput style had given rise to a mellifluous and romantic style of manuscript illustration. Among the most popular texts were those describing the youthful exploits and loves of Kṛṣṇa, such as the *Bhāgavata-Purāṇa* and *Gīta-Govinda*, and poetical treatments of the emotions of idealised lovers (often personified as Kṛṣṇa and his mistress Rādhā), such as the *Rasikapriyā* of Keśav Dās and the *Sat Saī* of Bihārī Lāl. Through the mobility of the artist families the new style soon became widespread throughout the Hills, though its classic phases are associated particularly with the courts of Guler and Kangra. By the early 19th century the first inspiration had waned and the sweetness of the style had started to become cloying and mannered.

This Garhwal painting from a series of the *Sat Saī* shows signs of the transition. The subject is a typical literary conceit (Ratnākar ed., no.405): Kṛṣṇa, overcome by love, has enshrined the tender maiden (Rādhā) in his heart and now discards his flower garland and camphor and sandal-paste unguents, lest their weight should oppress her. The cast-off garland lies on the carpet before him and the maidservant's sandal-crushing board remains unused. Kṛṣṇa gazes away in distraction while the two maids exchange a wondering glance. This treatment of the theme is evidently later in date than the version published by Randhawa, being more stiffly and nervously executed.

PUBLISHED

J.C. Harle, *The Art and Architecture of the Indian Sub-Continent*, London, 1986, fig.332; see also M.S. Randhawa, *Kangra Paintings of the Bihārī Sat Saī*, New Delhi, 1966, fig.6, p.18; Spink and Son, *Painting for the Royal Courts of India*, London, 1976, no.157.

94

COLOUR PLATE 20

A Sarus crane, gouache on paper. By Shaikh Zain ud-Dīn, Calcutta, c.1780–82

$37 \times 23\frac{1}{4}$ in. (94 × 59.5 cm.)

Radcliffe Science Library Loan

With the decline of the Mughal nobility in the later 18th century, many artists at the courts of eastern India and elsewhere began to turn for patronage to the new British ruling class. Much of the enormous output of these "Company" painters (see no.95)

consists of standardised series of illustrations of native castes and professions, festivals and monuments, which are sometimes little more than a superior form of tourist art. In a few cases, however, painters of real distinction formed a productive relationship with individual British patrons. One early example is Shaikh Zain ud-Dīn, who was employed for several years as a bird and animal artist by Mary, Lady Impey, wife of the first Chief Justice at Fort William, Sir Elijah Impey.

The Impeys had arrived in Calcutta in 1774 and soon came to share the fascination with India and the scientific curiousity about its life and culture which prevailed among members of the circle of Warren Hastings. While Sir Elijah collected Oriental manuscripts and paintings, Lady Impey formed a large menagerie of birds and animals, including some exotic specimens brought from further East. A series of meticulous studies of these living models, in most cases life-sized, was made by three artists in her employ. The most skilful and prolific of these was Shaikh Zain ud-Dīn; his two Hindu colleagues, Bhawānī Dās and Rām Dās, were responsible for less than a quarter of the known paintings. All three are described in the clerk's inscriptions which appear on many of the pages as "native of Patna", and it is likely that they had originally been trained there in the current Provincial Mughal style of painting. But even in the earliest paintings from the series (dated 1777) Zain ud-Dīn shows complete assurance in adapting his technique to the conventions of British natural history painting and the unfamiliar large format of the imported Whatman paper, while retaining much of the vitality of characterisation of the Indian tradition. This probably somewhat later study of a Sarus crane is remarkable for the fine delineation and subtle colouring of the bird's grey and brown plumage and its head and spindly crimson legs.

Work on the series ended prematurely when Sir Elijah was recalled to England in 1783, and in 1810, following his death, the collection was dispersed at auction in London. Of more than two hundred paintings in the series, about 120 are now known to survive, most of them bird studies. A group of eighteen of these is on loan to the Museum from the Radcliffe Science Library, Oxford, to which they were given in the 19th century by Sir Henry Acland. Fourteen of the pictures are by Zain ud-Dīn, three by Rām Dās and one by Bhawānī Dās.

95
A lapidary at work, gouache on paper. Patna (Company) school, c.1810. Attributed to Sewak Rām

Height $5\frac{1}{2}$ in. (14 cm.) Width $7\frac{1}{2}$ in. (19 cm.)
1966.232

An East India Company factory had long been established at Patna on the river Ganges in the late 18th century, and as the British strengthened their hold over northern India from Bengal, the city became an important administrative centre. A number of Indian artists, deprived of their traditional patronage by the Mughal nobility, migrated elsewhere (no.94), while others came to settle in Patna and began selling series of vignettes of Indian life in a Europeanised style to foreign residents and visitors in search of the picturesque. Sewak Rām (c.1770–c.1830), one of the earliest of these migrants, came from Murshidabad and by the turn of the 19th century had a successful bazaar shop specialising in sets of paintings of Indian trades, costumes and festivals. He was a conscientious artist, working in a sombre palette attuned to the British taste, who did much to establish the pictorial conventions of the Patna school (see also no.97). This study of a lapidary seated on a *darī*, cutting precious stones with a bow-drill, is one of two pictures attributed to Sewak Rām in the Museum's collection.

LITERATURE

M. Archer, *Patna Painting*, London, 1947, pp.17–18, pls.1–4; M. Archer, *Company Drawings in the India Office Library*, London, 1972, pp.98–99.

96 COLOUR PLATE 21

Śakuntalā writing a love-letter on a lotus leaf, oils on canvas, by Ravi Varma, c.1880–85

$35\frac{1}{2} \times 26\frac{3}{4}$ in. (90 × 65 cm.)
X.2502

After the dissolution of the East India Company and the establishment of direct British rule in 1858, an accelerating process of Westernisation took place in Indian urban culture. Following the earlier recommendations of Macaulay, higher education was modelled on English lines, and in many of the major cities Schools of Art were founded to inculcate European academic standards. Even in the nominally independent princely states the traditional arts suffered a final decline as their royal patrons emulated the tastes of the British. Among the new admirers of Western painting was the Maharaja of the southern state of Travancore (now Kerala), who patronised both European artists and Indians trained in the new techniques. His most famous and influential protegé was Raja Ravi Varma (1848–1906), who himself came from a princely family and married one of the Maharaja's sisters. In his youth he had been schooled by his uncle in the Company-influenced Tanjore style, but he quickly changed to oil painting after receiving some instruction from other artists at the court. For the most part he was self-taught, developing his style from the study of reproductions of works by European painters, including those of Bouguereau. His fame began to spread in the 1870s, when he twice won the Governor's gold medal at the Madras Exhibition. His second prize-winning picture, in 1878, was a more elaborate treatment of the present theme, depicting Śakuntalā, the heroine of Kālidāsa's classical drama, as a buxom maiden reclining on the ground as she writes her letter to her neglectful royal lover. It was purchased by the Governor, the Duke of Buckingham, who also commissioned a portrait of himself from the artist. Thereafter Ravi Varma became best known for his treatments of classical and epic subjects, which were generally rendered in a sentimental and theatrical manner and often executed with the assistance of members of his family. Later these heavy-handed Victorian visions of Indian mythology became ubiquitous in the form of mass-produced oleographs, of which the Museum has a substantial collection.

The present painting is an early and restrained example of Ravi Varma's mythological style, one of several treatments which he made of the Śakuntalā theme. It is believed to have been given to the Indian Institute in the 1880's by the Maharaja of Baroda, one of the artist's most important patrons. Monier-Williams published a colour reproduction of it by W. Griggs as the frontispiece to the fifth edition of his translation of *Śakuntalā* in 1887. Śakuntalā, the beautiful foster-daughter of a forest hermit, who has met the king on a hunting expedition and fallen in love with him, is here shown, in the third Act of the play, pining for him and, at the instigation of her two companions, writing a love-letter to him on a lotus leaf. (The King, who has been eavesdropping, thereupon reveals himself and the couple declare their love; afterwards, following a long separation caused by an ascetic's curse, they are in the end united.)

Śakuntalā, who is the most strongly painted of the three figures, gazes demurely in thought as she composes the letter, exhibiting little of the consuming passion evoked in Kālidāsa's verses. This decorous creature most of all suggests the banality of Ravi Varma's conception. Nevertheless, while today it is perhaps his portrait paintings that we can most admire, Ravi Varma's whole oeuvre has to be taken into account in any study of the development of modern painting in India.

PUBLISHED

Sir M. Monier-Williams tr., *Śakoontala, or the Lost Ring*, 5th ed., London, 1887, frontispiece; compare S.N. Joshi, *Half-tone Reprints of the Renowned Pictures of the late Raja Ravivarma*, Poona, 1911, pls.30, 31.

97 COLOUR PLATE 22

Kṛṣṇa and Rādhā, water-colour on paper, by Ishwari Prasad, c.1910

Height $7\frac{1}{8}$ in. (18 cm.) Width 5 in. (12.7 cm.)
X.2030

By the beginning of this century the old styles of Indian court painting had all but disappeared. The first developments of a recognisably Indian modern school were taking place in Bengal, where a group of artists associated with the Calcutta School of Art under E.B. Havell (Principal, 1896–1906) were turning away from the Western academicism represented by Ravi Varma's work (no.96) and were seeking to achieve a new synthesis based partly on indigenous traditions. The most influential of these painters was Abanindranath Tagore (nephew of the poet Rabindranath), who pioneered the eclectic "neo-Bengal" style, with its borrowings from European and Japanese art as well as the Ajanta wall-paintings and later Indian miniature painting. The subject matter typically consisted of somewhat sentimental renderings of mythological, literary and historical themes.

While many of the members of this new school belonged to the urban intelligentsia of Calcutta, Ishwari Prasad (1870–1950) was a notable exception. According to information recorded in the Havell papers at Santiniketan, he was descended from a line of Mughal and Company artists who had worked at the court of the emperor Muhammad Shāh (1719–48) and later at the provincial centres of Lucknow, Murshidabad and Patna. In his youth Ishwari Prasad was trained in the Patna Company style (no.95) by his grandfather Shiva Lal, one of the leading 19th century artists. Lacking adequate patronage, he went to Calcutta, where he was discovered by Havell drawing patterns for a European textile-importing firm. He is also said to have been employed as a lithographer and worked for Abanindranath Tagore in this role. With Havell's help he joined the staff of the Calcutta Art School in 1904 and painted there in a wide range of styles, from pure neo-Bengal to an archaistic Patna manner.

This water-colour painting of Kṛṣṇa playing his flute, enthroned with Rādhā on a stone plinth set in a luxuriant, craggy landscape, is a skilful imitation of Abanindranath's style. It is interesting to contrast it with one of Ishwari Prasad's more old-fashioned works, an unpublished painting in the Indian Museum, Calcutta, depicting Śiva on Mount Kailāsa with Nandī below him and Pārvatī standing with a garland in her raised hand (both pictures are signed: *Īśvarī*, in *devanāgarī* script). Although there are clear similarities between the two compositions, the Calcutta picture, with its conventional figures and rocky landscape with diminutive trees, is rooted in the late Provincial Mughal tradition. It is revealing that when Ishwari Prasad retired to Patna in his old age he preferred once again to work in a version of the local Company style of which he was the last living exponent.

LITERATURE

M. Archer, *Patna Painting*, London, 1947, p.33; M. Archer, *Company Drawings in the India Office Library*, London, 1972, p.101.

98 COLOUR PLATE 19

Casket, wood overlaid with mother-of-pearl in lac. Gujarat, c.1590–1600

Height $8\frac{1}{2}$ in. (21.6 cm.) Width $12\frac{1}{3}$ in. (31.4 cm.)
Depth $7\frac{1}{2}$ in. (19 cm.)
1980.146
Purchased with the help of the Friends of the Ashmolean

The production of wooden furniture decorated with overlaid pieces of iridescent mother-of-pearl set in dark lac was an important luxury handicraft of Western India in the 16th and 17th centuries. Examples of the technique survive in India in the cenotaph canopies at three tombs of Sufi Shaikhs, two of them at Ahmedabad and the other in the shrine of Nizām ud-Dīn Auliyā' at Delhi. However, much of the production was intended for export to foreign markets, including Ottoman Turkey and Europe. The approximately thirty surviving examples include a throne, a book-rest, pen-boxes, writing-chests and a number of caskets with bevelled lids. One of the latter, in Dresden, has an inventory date of 1602 and displays a very similar spade-shaped tree device to the present casket, which in spite of a slight coarseness in its decoration can therefore be dated to just before 1600. Its sides are decorated with medallions containing stylised interlaced foliate decoration, interspersed with palm trees and leafy fronds. The flat surface of the lid is executed in a similar style, but its sloping sides have geometric ornament of repeated hexagons and diamonds characteristic of Ottoman work, and it has been suggested that the casket was probably made for the Ottoman market. The chinoiserie base is a later replacement.

PUBLISHED

Spink and Son Ltd., *Islamic Art from India*, London, 1980, fig.88; Victoria and Albert Museum, *The Indian Heritage; Court Life and Arts under Mughal Rule*, Exhib. Cat., London, 1982, no.551; O. Impey, "Japanese Export Lacquer of the Seventeenth Century", Percival David Foundation Colloquies no.11, London, 1982, pl.2B; S. Digby, "The Mother-of-pearl Overlaid Furniture of Gujarat: the Holdings of the Victoria and Albert Museum", in R. Skelton *et al.* eds., *Facets of Indian Art*, London, 1986; S. Digby, *The Mother-of-pearl Overlaid Furniture of Gujarat: an Indian Handicraft of the Sixteenth and Seventeenth centuries*, (in press).

99 COLOUR PLATE 23

Scrutore (writing cabinet), painted and lacquered wood. Sind (?), early 17th century

Height 20 cm. (8 in.) Width 28.5 cm. ($11\frac{1}{4}$ in.)
Depth 21.5 cm. ($8\frac{1}{2}$ in.)
1978.129

Lacquer painting was an important luxury art in Safavid and Qajar Persia and Mughal India, being used especially for fine book-bindings made for royal patrons. As with many of the Mughal decorative arts, very few early examples now survive. This painted and lacquered *scrutore*, or small portable writing cabinet, is one of only two known examples of its type.

Drop-front caskets of this kind probably first appeared in Germany after the middle of the 16th century and soon became popular in Italy, the Iberian peninsula and elsewhere. Before 1600 examples were being made in Japan and India after models supplied by the Portuguese. The commonest Indian type of *scrutore* is teak-veneered with ivory inlay; examples in other techniques are much rarer.

The four sides of the cabinet are decorated with spirited scenes of noblemen in Mughal dress on caparisoned horses hunting various wild beasts, including deer, lion, tiger, fox and crane. The figures are finely painted in a restricted, earthy palette, generously heightened with gold, which is also used profusely on the surrounding large and exuberantly burgeoning shrubs and trees, creating dramatic

contrasts with the black background. The top has been restored and weakly repainted in a more Persianate style, probably in the 19th century.

The cabinet has been attributed by two authorities to the Deccan on stylistic grounds, but more recently it has been assigned to the Western province of Sind, which was a major centre for the manufacture of cabinets as well as painted and lacquered bows in the early 17th century.

PUBLISHED

M. Zebrowski, "Indian Lacquerwork and the Antecedents of the Qajar Style", *Colloquies on Art and Archaeology in Asia*, no.11, London, Percival David Foundation, 1982, pp.334–35, pl.1a–d; Victoria and Albert Museum, *The Indian Heritage: Court Life and Arts under Mughal Rule*, Exhib. Cat., London, 1982, no.544 (see also no.545); S. Digby, 'The mother-of-pearl overlaid furniture of Gujarat', fig.11, in R. Skelton et al., eds., *Facets of Indian art*, London, 1986.

100 COLOUR PLATE 24

Floral carpet, wool pile (780 knots per square inch), silk warps and wefts. Mughal, Lahore or Agra, early 18th century

Length $82\frac{3}{4}$ in. (210.8 cm.) Width 58 in. (147.3 cm.)
1975.17
Purchased with help of the beneficiaries of Sir David

Ross, the Friends of the Ashmolean and the Victoria & Albert Museum Purchase Grant Fund

The art of carpet-weaving developed among the nomadic peoples of Central Asia and was not indigenous to India, whose climate discouraged the use of woollen pile rugs as floor coverings. The manufacture of carpets probably began under the early Mughal emperors, especially Akbar, who, according to Abu'l Fazl in the *'Āīn-i Akbarī*, "has caused carpets to be made of wonderful varieties and charming textures; he has appointed experienced workmen, who have produced many masterpieces... All kinds of carpet-weavers have settled here, and drive a flourishing trade. They are found in every town, but especially in Agra, Fatehpur and Lahore." Akbar's weavers probably came from Herat (in modern Afghanistan), and the Persian influence on Mughal carpet design remained strong during the 17th century, when many of the finest examples were produced, although overlaid by the characteristic Mughal taste for bold floral decoration which developed under Jahāngīr and Shāh Jahān. By the 18th century designs were becoming more rigid, but a high level of technical quality remained.

The repeating floral pattern of this very well preserved and finely knotted rug, with its symmetrical groups of flowers and serrated lancet leaves on a dark wine-red ground, derives from a classical Herati model. The border of lotus buds and flowers, however, is of Indian inspiration; the same design is found on two similar rugs in the Metropolitan Museum, New York, and another which was sold at Christie's in 1981.

PUBLISHED

Victoria & Albert Museum, *The Indian Heritage: Court Life and Arts under Mughal Rule*, Exhib. Cat., London, 1982, no.204; D. Piper, *Treasures of the Ashmolean Museum*, Oxford, 1985, no.40.

101

Mirror-back, pale green jade inset with precious stones. Mughal, Delhi, early 19th century

Height 9¼ in. (23.7 cm.) Width 8¼ in. (21 cm.)
X.2327

Although the art of hardstone carving had been practised in India from an early period, it reached a peak of artistic and technical achievement under the Mughal emperors. Jade in particular had long been prized by their Central Asian forebears for its qualities of hardness, translucency, and delicacy of colouring, and the emperor Jahāngīr is known to have possessed several Timurid pieces. In the reign of Shāh Jahān, a lover of precious stones and of an icily perfect mar-

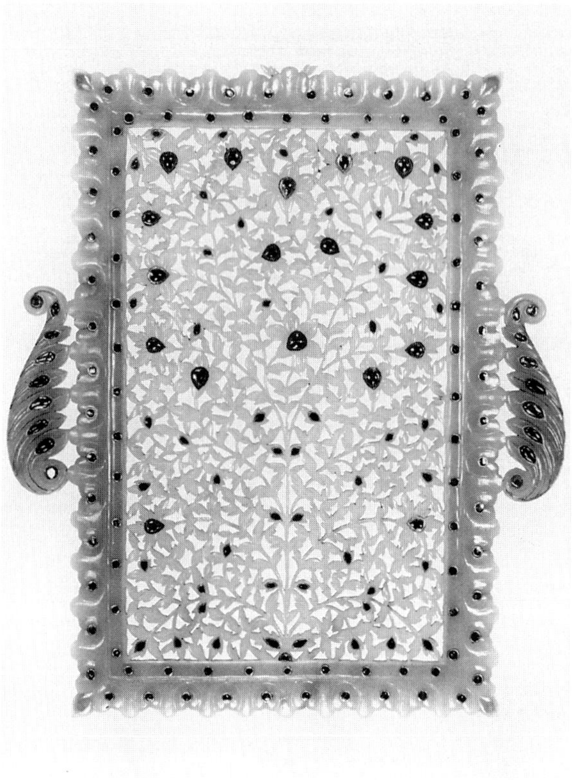

moreal architecture as embodied in the Tāj Mahal, many of the finest Mughal jades were carved. These often display the characteristic floral ornament of the period in low relief. In other objects, such as boxes, *huqqa* bases and dagger hilts, the jade surfaces were opulently patterned with small pieces of ruby, emerald and semi-precious stones inset in gold surrounds.

This mirror-back was made towards the end of the Mughal period, when the craftsmen were repeating the designs of the two previous centuries with diminishing virtuosity. It follows the rectangular shape of European mirrors which were imported in great numbers from the 17th century (Indian mirrors were traditionally round or oval). The intricate openwork carving of multiple branching flowers emanating from a central stem is in effect a miniature version of the pierced stonework *jālī* panels found in the window apertures and balustrades of the old Mughal palaces.

102

Head of the Virgin, ivory. Goa(?), 17th century

Height 9¾ in. (24.8 cm.) including stand
1963.181
Bouch Bequest

In the 16th century the Portuguese became the first Europeans to establish themselves in India, controll-

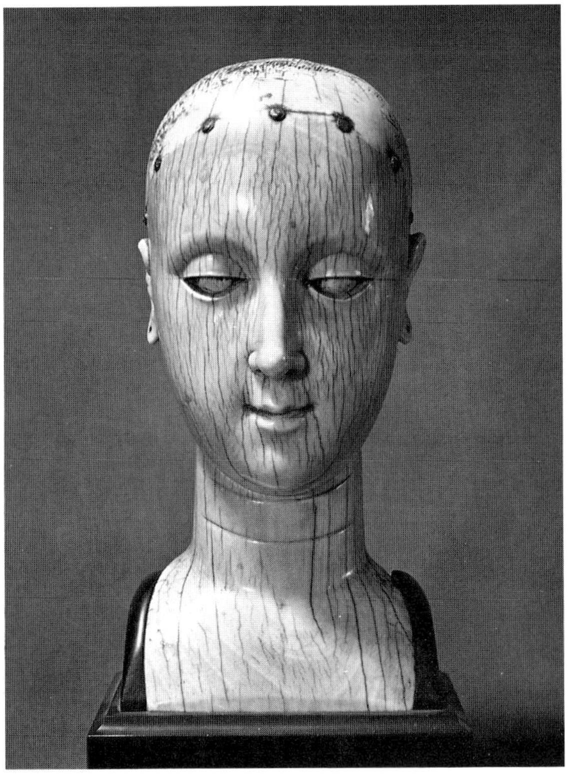

ing their Eastern trading empire from Goa, on India's west coast, which they had captured in 1510. The resident Portuguese intermarried freely with the local population and zealously converted them to Catholicism. The old town of Goa rang with the bells of numerous churches, monasteries, convents and seminaries, and pilgrims gathered at the shrine of the great missionary St. Francis Xavier (d. 1552). Long after the decline of Portuguese power, Goa's Christian culture has flourished to the present day.

Among local worshippers, themselves former Hindus, images of Jesus and Mary were much in demand. The Virgin in particular was revered as a saviour from disasters and protectress of seafarers. Figures in wood and ivory were at first imported from Europe but later produced in considerable numbers by local craftsmen, in some cases with distinctly Indian iconographic features. This finely carved head of Mary is of a type that has also been attributed to Far Eastern Catholic settlements such as Manila and Macao. Her head, which shows less patina at the top, would originally have been adorned with a suitable head-covering. Traces of red colouring remain on the lips. A comparable Goanese head is in the Prince of Wales Museum, Bombay (Desai, *loc. cit.*), and other examples are in private collections.

LITERATURE

K.P. Desai, "Icons of Faith", *Goa: An Encounter*, *Marg*, XXXV, 3, 1984, fig. 11.

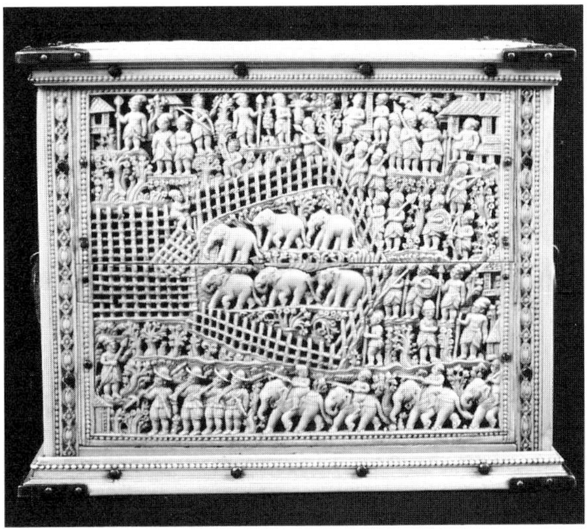

103

Cabinet, wood mounted with ivory. Ceylon (Sri Lanka), mid to late 17th century

Height $7\frac{1}{4}$ in. (18.5 cm.) Length 9 ins. (23 cm.)
Width 6 ins. (15.5 cm.)
1976.6
Purchased with the help of the Friends of the Ashmolean

In the 17th century the vigorous and highly organised Dutch East India Company built up an unrivalled Asian trading network which included a near-monopoly of the lucrative spices of Indonesia. As part of this commercial empire the Dutch established a number of trading posts in India and in the coastal regions of Ceylon, from which the last Portuguese stronghold had been removed by 1658. In Ceylon

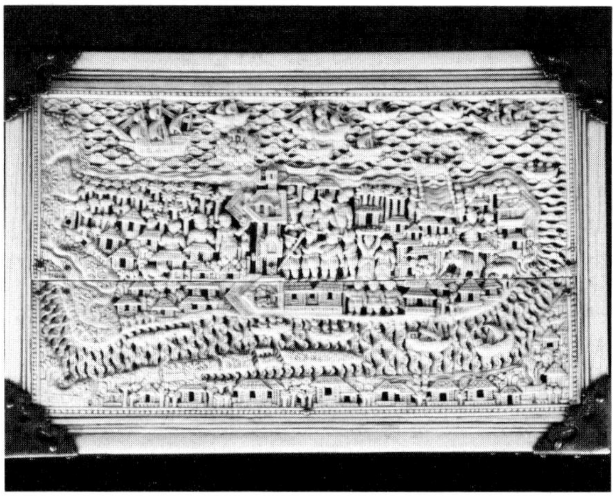

they were able to take advantage of the ancient indigenous traditions of wood and ivory-carving. Considerable quantities of hardwood furniture were produced after Dutch models, similar to the work associated with the Company's headquarters of Batavia (modern Jakarta), as seen for example in two carved ebony chairs said to have been owned by Charles II's queen Catherine of Braganza, which came to the Museum from Elias Ashmole in 1683.

The ivory carvers of Ceylon were already accustomed to producing fine pieces in the European (Portuguese) taste as export or presentation items, as is shown by a small surviving group of elaborate caskets incorporating Christian and European imagery which date from the mid-16th century. The Museum's cabinet is a similarly hybrid production, although of a later type. It is overlaid with carved ivory panels, mingling scenes of Europeans with traditional decoration. The top panel shows the reception of a European party among the huts and palms of a port in Ceylon, with several ships riding at anchor among billowing waves. The back panel depicts the culmination of an elephant hunt, with six elephants penned in a stockade and four European soldiers among the participants. The two sides of the cabinet are decorated with intricate foliated scrollwork, with a pair of flying parrots, around a central lotus rosette. The door panels have pairs of fiercely strutting *śerapendiyas* (or *śarapendās*), a lion-headed variant of the auspicious *haṁsa* bird which is a common motif in the later ivory and metalwork of Ceylon. The five internal drawers are decorated in a similar style.

104

Cabinet, wood mounted with ivory. Coromandel coast (South India) or Ceylon, late 17th or early 18th century

Height 19$\frac{3}{4}$ in. (50.1 cm.) Length 25$\frac{5}{8}$ ins. (65 cm.)
Width 16$\frac{3}{8}$ in. (41.7 cm.)
Mrs. M. Combe Bequest; transferred from Department of Western Art
1981.47

Like no.103, this larger ivory cabinet would have been made for a European (probably Dutch) patron, at one of the trading settlements on the Coromandel coast or in Ceylon. Furniture of this type was made for everyday use rather than export, but a number of examples were brought to Europe as gifts or by retiring Company officers returning home. The top, side and door panels are made up of multiple ivory plaques carved in low relief with a bold floral meander pattern. The inner sides of the doors and the eight internal drawers are similarly decorated. The luxuriant large-headed flower decoration is much closer to the

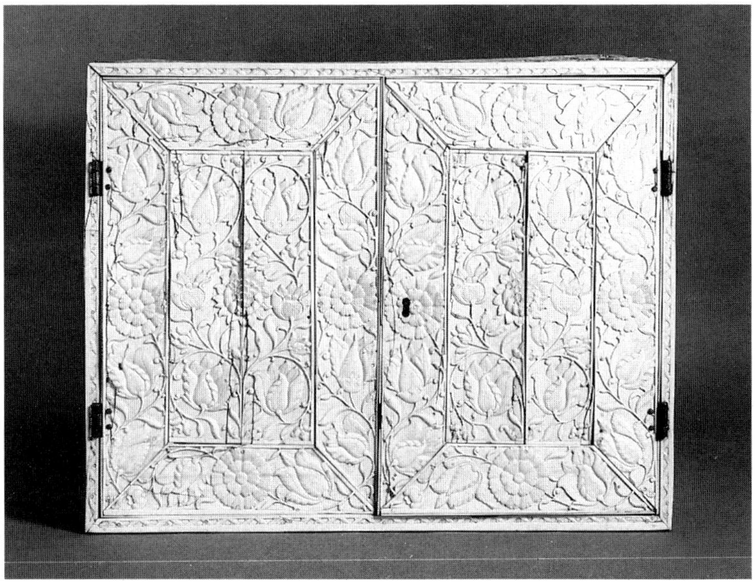

European taste than to the sparer, more formal Mughal floral ornament of northern India.

A larger and more elaborately carved ivory cabinet of similar type, now in the Victoria and Albert Museum (I.S. 70-1959), formerly belonged to the artist William Holman Hunt (1827–1910). It is reported that the present cabinet was also found by Holman Hunt in London, and was purchased on his advice by Mrs. Combe, who later bequeathed it to the Museum. An ivory box in a comparable decorative style is in the Archaeological Museum, University of Peradeniya, Sri Lanka (van Lohuizen-de Leeuw, *loc. cit.*).

LITERATURE

J. van Lohuizen-de Leeuw, *Sri Lanka: Ancient Arts*, London, 1981, fig.89.

105

A Dutchman, painted and lacquered wood. Gujarat, first half of 18th century

Height 35 in. (89 cm.) including stand
1968.42

This painted, half life-sized figure of a European is flat and unfinished at the back and may once have formed a decorative fixture in the palace of a nobleman of Western India; it has later been mounted as a free-standing sculpture on a rectangular stand. The subject is most likely modelled on the Dutch East India Company officers who resided in some numbers at Surat in the late 17th and early 18th centuries and travelled from there to Agra and the U.P. region to buy textiles and indigo. This Dutchman wears a typical red coat, with the addition of an Indian floral pattern, and with yellow trimming and large pockets on the outside. He is red-lipped and his periwig, carved with pronounced curls, was formerly black.

Figures of *firangīs* ("Franks", or Europeans) began to appear as exotic decorative features in the 18th century, for example in the palace buildings at Udaipur in Rajasthan and at Bhuj in Kutch. The latter became an important centre of European artistic influence, due to the innovations of the legendary Rām Siṅgh Malam, "the Navigator", who is said to have thrice visited Europe and introduced a wide range of Western technical skills on his return.

106

a) Ceremonial swing for an image of Kṛṣṇa, painted, lacquered and gilded wood with glass, foil and mirrorwork. Rajasthan, late 19th century

Height $5\frac{1}{2}$ ft. (154 cm.)
1968.43

b) The swinging of the deity, gouache with silver and gold on paper. Kotah, Rajasthan, c.1850

Height $8\frac{1}{2}$ in. (22.1 cm.) Width $6\frac{1}{2}$ in. (16.2 cm.)
1966.230

Swinging in the open air was from early times a popular spring pastime in India and is described in Sanskrit literature as an occasion for lovers' dalliance. It was also a pleasant way of keeping cool in the summer heat, and rows of hooks for swing-beds can still be seen in the ceilings of old Rajput palaces. In the Mughal period the image of a prince or noble couple seated enjoyably in a swing was incorporated in the *rāgamālā* iconography (see no.88) for Hindola ("swing") *rāga*.

This typical royal pastime also became part of the *pūjā* (devotional) ceremonies of various religious cults, most notably in Rajasthan in the cult of Śrī Nāthjī, a form of Kṛṣṇa, whose main shrine is at Nathdwara, a small town to the north of Udaipur. The daily worship

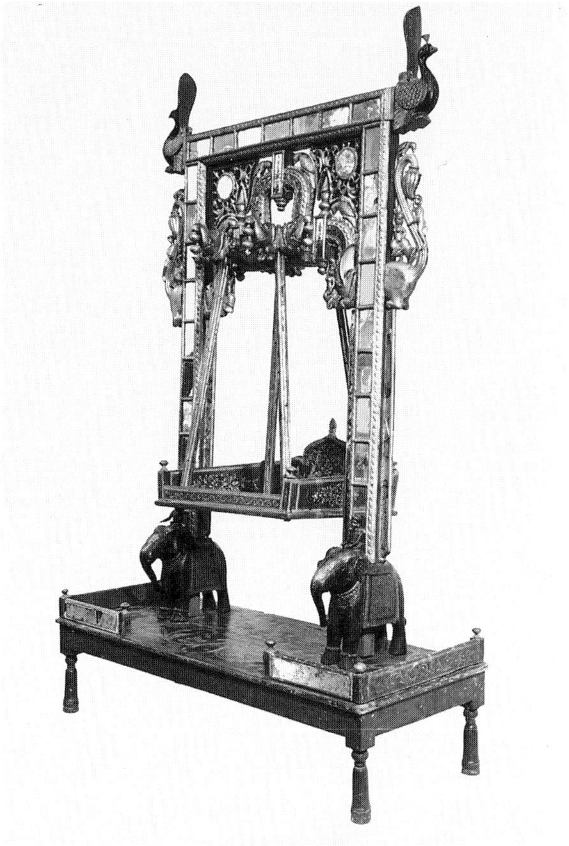

at the temple follows an elaborate prescribed ritual of waking and bathing the deity, clothing him like a prince, offering him fine meals and putting him to sleep again. At set hours the worshippers are admitted to watch the ceremonies and have *darśan* ("vision") of the god. During the year there are also twenty-four major seasonal festivals with their own special rituals, which in several cases include seating the garlanded deity in a swing, as can be seen in a 19th century painting (106b), in which three small gold images of manifestations of Kṛṣṇa are gently rocked by a priest.

The wooden frame of the Museum's swing (106a) is inlaid with mirror plaques and supported by caparisoned elephants with mahouts. It terminates in peacock finials and intersects a pair of *makaras* (with associated *apsarases*, monkeys and parrots), from whose mouths issues the *toraṇa* arch (with parrots and scrollwork) from which the swing is suspended. The struts of the swing terminate in multiple *makara* heads with hanging bobbles, and its seat is painted with birds and floral scrollwork on a red ground. A small portrait of a Vaiṣṇava saint seated in *padmāsana* on a tiger skin is set into the centre of the leading cross-beam of the swing itself. The wooden stand is also painted red with scrolling vegetal decoration in yellow and green. The top is missing.